Hebrews

60 Biblical Insights by **Robert M. Solomon**

Journey Through Hebrews
© 2018 by Robert M. Solomon
Published by Discovery House Publishing Singapore Pte. Ltd.
All rights reserved.

Discovery House Publishing™ is affiliated
with Our Daily Bread Ministries Asia Ltd.

Requests for permission to quote
from this book should be directed to:

Permissions Department
Our Daily Bread Publishing
P. O. Box 3566
Grand Rapids, MI 49501, USA

Or contact us by email at
permissionsdept@odb.org

All websites listed are accurate at the time of publication, but may change in the
future or cease to exist. The listing of the website references does not imply our
endorsement of the site's entire contents.

Design by Joshua Tan
Typeset by Grace Goh

ISBN 978-1-62707-840-5

Foreword

Apart from the last two chapters, many readers find the book of Hebrews difficult to understand. This is because the author is writing to Jewish Christians and makes numerous references to their former Jewish beliefs and practices, not to encourage the believers to remain in them but to dissuade these Christians from being tempted to leave their faith and return to their former religion.

Though reading and understanding Hebrews may be a little challenging, spending time studying it carefully rewards readers with deep insights and rich spiritual blessings. Here you will find a majestic and inspiring view of Jesus, who is fully God and fully man. The aspect of Jesus most substantially portrayed in Hebrews is that of a unique and irreplaceable High Priest. In offering himself as a sacrifice for our sins, He has secured for us a great salvation through the shedding of His precious blood. Here we will meet Him as the author and perfecter of our faith, the God who became man to die for us and empathises with us in our journey on earth, who is coming again to judge and, as our eternal High Priest, to offer eternal rest for those who would believe in Him.

Come; let us meet Him in the pages of this wonderful epistle, written not only for Christians long ago, but also for us today. May the Holy Spirit lead us to understand the God who still speaks today.

All Glory to Him,
Robert M. Solomon

We're glad you've decided to join us on a journey into a deeper relationship with Jesus Christ!

The *Journey Through* series is designed to help believers spend time with God in His Word, book by book. Each title is written by a faithful Bible teacher to help you read, reflect, and apply God's Word, a little bit at a time. It's a great accompaniment to be read alongside the Bible, as you dig deeper into God's Word. We trust the meditation on God's Word will draw you into a closer relationship with Him through our Lord and Saviour, Jesus Christ.

How to use this resource

READ: After reading and reflecting on the Bible verses, use the explanatory notes to help you understand the Scriptures in fresh ways.

REFLECT: Use the questions to consider how you could respond to God and His Word, letting Him change you from the inside out.

RECORD: Jot down your thoughts and responses in the space provided to keep a diary of your journey with the Lord.

An Overview

According to many scholars, the book of Hebrews was written to a group of second-generation Jewish Christians who were facing growing persecution. No one knows for sure who the author was. He was most likely a Jewish Christian who wrote just before the destruction of Jerusalem and its temple by the Romans in AD 70.

At that time, the Jews were exempted from rituals involving emperor worship, but not the Christians, who faced severe persecution if they refused to participate. Many Jewish Christians were tempted to return to Judaism to avoid persecution, but the writer urges them to stay true to Christ. He does this by showing them why Christ is "better" (the word occurs 13 times)[1] than angels, Moses and his law, the old priesthood, and the animal sacrifices in the old sanctuary. The author uses many Old Testament quotations to argue his point; most of these are attributed directly to God without mention of human intermediaries.[2] To trust and follow Christ is not to follow an entirely new religion, but to recognise that He is the fulfilment of all that was promised by the old covenant. It would therefore be foolish to leave the redemptive reality of Christ and return to what is merely the representative shadow of the old religion.

Imagine an aged parent still clinging to the tattered photograph of her long-lost son even after he finally returns home. Wouldn't it be strange if she was unable to differentiate the profound difference between the old photograph and the living person? Such is the writer's argument to show that Jesus is the perfect Lawgiver and sympathetic High Priest who shed His blood on the cross to save us. Far from drifting away from Christ, we should draw near to Him and hold on to Him with faith, faithfulness, and perseverance even amid persecution, for we have a great salvation only in Him who is the eternal anchor for our souls.

1 F. F. Bruce, *The Epistle to the Hebrews* (Grand Rapids: Eerdmans, 1964), 9.
2 W. H. Griffith Thomas, *Hebrews: A Devotional Commentary* (Grand Rapids: Eerdmans, 1987), 27.

Outline

1:1–4:13	The Supremacy of Christ
4:14–7:28	Christ the Perfect High Priest
8:1–10:39	The New and Better Covenant of Christ
11:1–40	The Great Heritage of Faith
12:1–13:19	Faithful Christian Living
13:20–25	Christ the Great Shepherd

Key Verse

We have come to share in Christ, if indeed we hold our original conviction firmly to the very end. —Hebrews 3:14

Glossary

Angels:
Supernatural beings who serve as heavenly messengers. Many first-century Jews were fascinated with angels and held them in high esteem, so the author of Hebrews establishes that the Son is superior even to them.

Aaron, Aaronic priesthood (Levitical priesthood, high priest):
From the Israelite tribe of Levi, God chose the descendants of Aaron, the older brother of Moses, to serve as priests in the tabernacle (and later the temple). The most important was the high priest, who alone was permitted to enter the Holy of Holies once a year on the Day of Atonement. The author of Hebrews contrasts this hereditary priesthood with the eternal priesthood of Christ.

Atonement, Day of Atonement:
Under covenant law, the priests had to perform animal (blood) sacrifices to seek God's forgiveness for the sins of the people. These sacrifices had to be repeated annually, most notably by the high priest on the Day of Atonement. This institution culminated in the death and resurrection of Jesus; no more sacrifices would be necessary for those who believed in Him.

Covenant (Old and New):
The old covenant was the agreement between God and the nation of Israel, setting them apart as His chosen people. They were expected to live according to His commandments; faithfulness would be rewarded, while disobedience would be judged and punished. With the death and resurrection of Jesus, a new covenant was made: those who believed in Him would have their sins forgiven, be made holy, and receive eternal life in heaven.

Faith:

In the Christian context, faith is to place our confidence in God's promises and to trust in Jesus totally for salvation rather than on our own strength. This confidence, or hope, results in a personal relationship with God that sets the priorities of our lives. In Hebrews, the author encourages readers to remember the hope that they have experienced in Jesus.

Holy of Holies:

The innermost room of the tabernacle (and later the temple), separated from the outside by a heavy curtain, where the ark of the covenant was kept, and where God would be present. Entry to this most sacred place was forbidden, except for the high priest once a year on the Day of Atonement. Jesus' sacrifice tore the separating curtain in two, opening a way for believers to enter the presence of God in the true Holy of Holies (heaven).

Law:

A body of commandments given by God through Moses to the nation of Israel, defining the covenantal relationship they were to have with Him. Obedience to the law became the foundation of Jewish life. See *covenant*.

Melchizedek:

The king of Salem (Jerusalem) and a priest of the Most High God during the time of Abraham, forefather of the Israelites. His name means "king of righteousness". Melchizedek provided refreshment and blessed the weary Abraham and his men after a great battle; Abraham acknowledged Melchizedek's priesthood by giving him a tithe (tenth) of the plunder. In Hebrews, the author presents Melchizedek as a type of Christ.

Mount Sinai:
A sacred mountain wreathed in smoke, fire, and thunder, where Moses received the law from God. It is used figuratively by the author of Hebrews to represent the old covenant.

Mount Zion:
A common name for the Temple Mount and Jerusalem itself. It is used figuratively by the author of Hebrews to represent the new covenant of grace found in Jesus Christ.

Sacrifice:
Covenant law required regular animal (blood) sacrifices as a symbol of God's forgiveness. The death and resurrection of Jesus ended the need for further sacrifices. See *atonement*.

Tabernacle (Temple):
Meaning "dwelling-place", the tabernacle was a temporary place of worship constructed by Moses on God's direction to house the ark of the covenant; King Solomon would eventually build the temple to replace it. The author of Hebrews stresses that the tabernacle (and later the temple) was built according to God's design as an earthly echo of the true tabernacle in heaven, where Jesus Christ serves as high priest.

Day 1

Read Hebrews 1:1-3

Hebrews begins "as dramatically as a rocket shot to the moon".[3] It gets straight to the point in declaring the divinity of Christ and His identity as Prophet, Priest, and King like no other.

Hebrews 1:1–3 gives us a crash course on Christology, teaching us the essential truths about Jesus. He is God's Son (v. 2), who was at the beginning when God made the universe through Him. He will also dominate the future because He is God's sole "heir of all things" (v. 2).[4] He is no less than God, for He is the "radiance of God's glory" (just as the Sun and its rays are intimately related) and the "exact representation of his being" (v. 3). The latter phrase is a translation of the Greek word for "character"—the printing tile that produces an exact reproduction of itself.[5] Jesus sustains all things with His powerful Word (v.3; see Colossians 1:17). He is fully divine.

The three key leadership roles in ancient Israel were that of prophet, priest, and king. The author demonstrates that Jesus fulfils all three offices in an amazing way. He is the Prophet above all prophets, for God spoke in the past through His prophets, but now He "has spoken to us by his Son" (Hebrews 1:2). In Jesus, we hear God's final and complete word. Jesus has also "provided purification for sins" (v. 3). The sacrifices that the priests had to do repeatedly, Jesus has now done in one pivotal act on the cross, where He offered himself as the "atoning sacrifice for our sins" (1 John 2:2). Having accomplished this for our salvation, Jesus took His rightful seat at the right hand of the Father. He reigns over all as the King of kings.

The author thus declares that there is no one like Jesus. **He is the Prophet who surpasses all prophets, the Priest who surpasses all priests, and the King who rules above all kings.** He is far above even the very best that Israel has produced in its long history. We should consider Him seriously.

[3] Ray C. Stedman, *Hebrews*, IVP New Testament Commentary Series (Downers Grove: InterVarsity Press, 1992), 19.
[4] Philip Edgcumbe Hughes, *A Commentary on the Epistle to the Hebrews* (Grand Rapids: Eerdmans, 1990), 39.
[5] Leon Morris, "Hebrews", in *The Expositors Bible Commentary*, ed. Frank E. Gaebelein, vol. 12 (Grand Rapids: Zondervan, 1981), 14.

Reflect on each piece of evidence in this passage on the divinity of Jesus. What is your response to what you have discovered or rediscovered? How would you explain to others why Jesus is fully divine?

Reflect on how Jesus is the incomparable Prophet, Priest, and King. How does He exercise these roles in your life?

Day 2

Read Hebrews 1:4–14

Yesterday, we looked at how Jesus is superior to anything the Jews have known in their religion thus far. Today's text shows how He is far superior to the angels of heaven. Angels are created beings and, apart from the fallen ones that followed Satan in his rebellion against God, are depicted as glorious creatures that serve God. But Jesus, being God the Son, is far superior to the angels. Unlike them, He is not a created being.

The author quotes several Old Testament passages to make his point. He begins with Psalm 2:7 where God tells Christ that He is His Son; such words were never addressed to any angel (Hebrews 1:5). Similarly, 2 Samuel 7:14 and 1 Chronicles 17:13 are referenced. The writer also quotes the Septuagint translation (the Greek translation of the Hebrew Bible) of Deuteronomy 32:43 ("Let all God's angels worship him") to show how all angels are to bow before Jesus (v. 6). Jesus is the "firstborn" because, as uncreated God, He exists before all creation.[6]

Angels are ministers and servants of God—like wind and fire—who do the bidding of God (Hebrews 1:7, quoting Psalm 104:4), but Jesus is far superior. He is addressed as God by God himself! God says to Christ, "Your throne, O God, will last for ever and ever" (Psalm 45:6–7) and refers to himself as "your God" (Hebrews 1:8–9). Without understanding the biblical doctrine of the Trinity, that there is one God eternally existing as the Father, Son, and Holy Spirit, we would be rather confused and puzzled.

The writer quotes Psalm 102:25–27 to show that Christ was present at the creation of the world, and remains unchanging from eternity to eternity (Hebrews 1:10–12; see 13:8). The writer also quotes Psalm 110:1, a favourite passage among New Testament writers (Matthew 22:44; Acts 2:34–35), to show the divinity of Christ (Hebrews 1:13). No angel comes close to such heights of majesty and divinity. While angels are heavenly beings and they serve God, it is wrong to focus on them over and above Christ. A fascination with angels existed among the Jews in the time of the New Testament; some elevated them as mediators to be worshipped (see Colossians 2:18). The writer points to Christ who is above all angels and our one mediator (1 Timothy 2:5; the Greek term for mediator is part of the legal language referring to an arbitrator)[7] who brings us to God directly.

[6]Bruce, *Epistle to the Hebrews*, 15.
[7]Morris, "Hebrews", 76.

Why do you think
the writer empha-
sised that Jesus
is vastly superior
to angels? Why is
both dismissal of
the existence and
ministry of angels
and unhealthy
fascination with them
unhelpful in the
Christian life?

How does the
truth that Jesus
is unchanging
throughout eternity
(Hebrews 1:12) and
that He is the begin-
ning and the end
(Hebrews 1:10–12;
Revelation 1:8, 17;
21:6) impact your
life today?

Day 3

Read Hebrews 2:1–4

Continuing the train of thought related to the superiority of Jesus above angels ("therefore", Hebrews 2:1), the writer argues that what we receive from Jesus is "so great a salvation" that it must not be ignored or belittled (v. 3). The Jews believed that the law of Moses was brought by angels (Hebrews 2:2; Acts 7:38, 53; Galatians 3:19). If obedience to this law was of prime importance, and the breaking of it justly punished, how much more important it is to obey the message brought by the Son of God, who is worshipped by angels. This message of salvation was "first announced by the Lord" (see Mark 1:15). It was He who announced the coming of His kingdom of grace and our need for faith and repentance. Jesus' declarations and teachings were "confirmed to us by those who heard him" (Hebrews 2:3), who were His witnesses (see Acts 1:8; 1 John 1:1). God also authenticated the message of Jesus (John 2:11; 5:36–37) and the apostles' testimony with "signs, wonders and various miracles, and by gifts of the Holy Spirit" (Hebrews 2:4; Acts 2:43; Romans 15:19).

The message of salvation announced and demonstrated by Jesus, culminating in the cross and the empty tomb, is of utmost importance because of who Jesus is.

We must therefore "pay the most careful attention" to what we have heard (Hebrews 2:1). For the readers of Hebrews, what they had heard would have been either apostolic preaching or testimonies of the apostles (which would eventually become the New Testament). Notice how closely they were to give attention to these things; the words "most careful" (v. 1) underline the quality of thought and response that was necessary. The apostle Peter echoes this point in 2 Peter 1:19 when he urges his readers to pay attention to the testimony concerning Christ in Scripture. By doing so, we will experience God's light shining in us through His Word, till Christ returns to shine perfectly in our hearts as a morning star brings a new day. We will thus be blessed.

There is danger in not giving Christ and His message sufficient attention. A person who fails to continue to listen to Christ (see Matthew 17:5) will "drift away" (*parerrein*, meaning "slip away from", Hebrews 2:1). The second-generation Jewish believers were in danger of rejecting Christ. Like them, we also risk losing our way when we neglect Christ. We must pay heed to this first of five warnings found in the book (see Hebrews 3:12–19; 6:4–8; 10:26–31; 12:25–29).

Consider what Jesus taught and said about himself in the Gospels. Why is this so important to the Christian life? Make a list of reasons why your salvation in Christ is great.

Reflect on how people drift away from Christ. Recall situations in your past experience where you may have drifted away. How did you find out, and what did you do to return to the Lord? How can you prevent yourself from drifting away from Christ?

Day 4

Read Hebrews 2:5–9

While Hebrews 1 focused on the divinity of Jesus, Hebrews 2:5–18 focuses on His humanity. Three points are made that show the significance of His humanity: He died for us (Hebrews 2:9), He pioneered our salvation (v. 10), and He is our present help in our struggles and temptations (v. 18). Hebrews 2:5–9 discusses how Jesus tasted death for everyone (v. 9). The author quotes Psalm 8:4–6 (vv. 6–8) to show the elevated position God originally gave the human race. Man was made "a little lower than the angels" and crowned with "glory and honour". God "put everything under their feet" (see Genesis 1:28). But this is no longer the case. Something has gone wrong. The cause is man's fall into sin and rebellion against God (Genesis 3). "All have sinned and fall short of the glory of God" (Romans 3:23).

This necessitated the coming of Jesus into the world as a human being. He was made "lower than the angels for a little while" (Hebrews 2:9), meaning that though He was God and fully divine, He chose to be born as a human being (Philippians 2:6–7). He identified with sinful humans, though He did not sin (Hebrews 4:15). He was thus able to take the place of us all on the cross, and accept the punishment intended for us. The "wages of sin is death" (Romans 6:23), a death that includes both physical death as well as eternal death. Jesus "suffered death" on the cross (Hebrews 2:9) on our behalf. It was not just the physical death that we will all have to experience eventually, but a far more devastating experience of death—the final separation from the gracious and loving God who created us, what the Bible calls the "second death" (Revelation 20:14).

Jesus became a man in order to take our place and "taste death for everyone" (Hebrews 2:9). Because He died for us, we can live in Him (2 Corinthians 5:15). Though we will die at the end of our earthly lives, we will be raised to new life in Christ (John 11:25; Ephesians 2:6). Jesus became a man to save us, and He is now above the angels, "crowned with glory and honour" (Hebrews 2:9), showing in His one person both the model human being as well as the Creator God (see Philippians 2:9–11). He is the God-Man who saves us.

What would have happened if Jesus was not born as a human being? What would have happened to you? What does it mean to live "without hope and without God in the world" (Ephesians 2:12)?

Reflect on what it meant for Jesus to taste death for you. Turn your thoughts to the praise and worship of Christ.

Day 5

Read Hebrews 2:10–13

The second reason why Jesus had to be made fully human was in order to chart a new course for human history and individual lives.

Jesus is identified as the *archēgos* (translated as "pioneer" or "author"; Hebrews 2:10). This great title is also used for Jesus elsewhere in Scripture (Acts 3:15; 5:31; Hebrews 12:2). It refers to one "who brings something in order that others may enter into it".[8] The default story of every human being is a sad one. We are born into sin, we sin, and we are eternally condemned. Jesus became a trailblazer ("pathfinder").[9] Like us, He was born into this world as a child. But unlike us all, though He was tempted in every way, He did not sin (Hebrews 4:15, 7:26–28, 10:14). Unlike Adam and Eve, our forebears, who sinned at a tree in the Garden of Eden (Genesis 3:6–7), Jesus died on a tree to save us (Acts 5:30; 10:39).

Jesus, as the new Adam (1 Corinthians 15:45), traced the major milestones of human life and charted a new course for human beings. Those who believe in Him will share the new story of the new Adam: we are born, we die, but we will be resurrected and will ascend to the heavenly realms (Ephesians 2:6). It is in this way that Jesus is the Pioneer of our salvation. Strangely, the author says that Jesus had to be made "perfect through what he suffered" (Hebrews 2:10). Does this mean that He had to be "improved" through suffering? The answer is no because in the next verse (v. 11), he is differentiated ("the one who makes people holy") from the rest of us ("those who are made holy"). Jesus did suffer for us on earth. In His sufferings, He shows that God is not a stranger to human suffering and perfectly identifies with His suffering creatures. Jesus is not made better by suffering, but we become better people because of suffering. For suffering "produces perseverance; perseverance, character; and character, hope" (Romans 5:3–4).

By suffering for and with us, Jesus saves us and shows His sympathy for our painful situation (Hebrews 2:17–18; 4:15–16; 5:7–10). He identifies with us ("of the same family"), calling us brothers and sisters (Hebrews 2:11; see Mark 3:35). The author quotes Psalm 22:22 (Hebrews 2:12) and Isaiah 8:17–18 (Hebrews 2:13) to reiterate his point.

[8] William Barclay, "The Letter to the Hebrews", in *The Daily Study Bible* (Edinburgh: St Andrews Press, 1992), 26.
[9] Bruce, *Epistle to the Hebrews*, 43.

ThinkThrough

What has Jesus done to change your story and destiny? Who did Jesus say are His brothers and sisters (Matthew 12:50)? What does it mean for Jesus to call you His brother or sister (v. 11)? What changes do you need to make in the light of your reflections?

How are we perfected through suffering? When we suffer, how can we follow in the steps of Jesus (1 Peter 2:21) and draw inspiration and comfort from Him?

Day 6

Read Hebrews 2:14–18

The third reason for the full humanity of Jesus, the Son of God, has to do with His solidarity with the human race and His empathy for us who are "flesh and blood" (Hebrews 2:14). He has shared in our humanity and walks with us though life with all its fears, trials, and darkness.

One of our deepest fears is that of death. Man has devised all kinds of religious practices to cope with this fear because he has no control over what lies beyond this life. The writer points out that it is the devil that has held people in bondage with their fear of death (Hebrews 2:14–15). He has either spread fake news about death and the unknown and locked people up in their superstitions, or deceived them into denying death (see Genesis 3:4). Jesus not only taught the truth about death, but also died for us and rose to life, thus conquering death for us. Through Him we discover the "death of death" and no longer need to be paralysed by the fear of death. **By walking with us, through death and beyond, Jesus allays all our fears.**

The humanity of Jesus is emphasised in the phrase "he had to be made like them, fully human in every way" (Hebrews 2:17). In this way, He becomes a "merciful and faithful high priest" who makes "atonement for the sins of the people" (v.17; see Romans 3:25). Besides dying for us, He also walks with us today so that we have the comfort of His presence and understanding. He is not a distant God unfamiliar with temptation or suffering, for "he himself suffered when he was tempted" (Hebrews 2:18). Like us, He was sorely tempted (see Matthew 4:1–11; Luke 4:1–13). But unlike us, He never sinned and overcame every temptation (Hebrews 4:15, 7:26–28).

He suffered various trials in His earthly life; He knew what it meant to be lonely (Matthew 26:40), weary (John 4:6), disappointed (Matthew 17:17), hungry (Matthew 21:18), grieving (John 11:35), falsely accused (Matthew 26:60–61), and face death without mercy and dignity (Luke 23:32–37). Thus, whenever we suffer, He looks at us with understanding eyes that say, "In this world you will have trouble. But take heart! I have overcome the world" (John 16:33). "Jesus went all the way for us."[10] There is simply no one like Jesus to "help those who are being tempted" (Hebrews 2:18).

[10] Morris, "Hebrews", 30.

How does knowing that Jesus went through all human trials and temptations provide comfort and strength for us?

Why is it important that Jesus is our merciful and faithful High Priest (Hebrews 2:17)? Tell Him how much you appreciate His humanity even as you worship Him as fully divine.

Day 7

Read Hebrews 3:1–6

Jesus is far superior not only to the angels, but also to Moses, who was highly revered by the Jews. While Jews honoured their forefathers such as Abraham, Isaac, and Jacob, they gave Moses a special place as the one who was given God's law for His people. As the author of the first five books of the Bible (the Book of the Law), he is recognised as the bringer of God's law to the Jews. Jesus is the prophet greater than Moses, whom Moses foretold in Deuteronomy 18:15 (Acts 3:22; John 1:45; 5:46; 6:14; 7:40). At the transfiguration, Moses appeared together with Elijah to talk with Jesus, and then disappeared. Jesus was left standing alone, peerless and unique (Matthew 17:1–8).

The point is emphasised in this passage. Jesus is "worthy of greater honour than Moses" (Hebrews 3:3). Moses was a highly respected servant of God whom God used to lead His people away from slavery in Egypt to the Promised Land and to bring them His law. But Moses was just a man; Jesus is more than that. Moses was faithful as a servant (v. 5; see Numbers 12:7–8), but Jesus claims authority as the faithful Son of God (Hebrews 3:6). Jesus is the divine lawgiver and the divine Deliverer who leads His people to freedom. Moses was part of God's fallen creation; part of the cosmic house, but Jesus is the creator and builder of that house (vv. 3–4). Thus, the difference between Moses and Jesus is the difference between a part of the house (say a pillar or beam) and the builder himself. **While the Jews can give Moses honour and respect, their response to Jesus must be entirely different.** Moses is part of God's house, just as we are (v. 6), but Christ has authority over Moses and us as the unique Son of God (v. 6) and builder of God's house (v. 3).

All this means that Christians must learn how to "fix [our] thoughts on Jesus" (Hebrews 3:1). Jesus is the "apostle", literally the One who was sent by the Father, and the "high priest", a theme that will be explained later in the book. For now, we simply note that being fully God and fully man, He is the perfect "bridge-builder" between righteous God and sinful man.[11] We are to fix our thoughts on Him (*katonoein* in Greek), meaning we are to consider everything carefully to discover the deep truth about Jesus.

[11] Barclay, "The Letter to the Hebrews", 31.

ThinkThrough

What does this passage say about the danger of elevating a Christian leader, institution, or programme above Christ?

How can you fix your thoughts on Jesus? What would it involve and why is it necessary to grow in our "heavenly calling" (Christian discipleship)?

Day 8

Read Hebrews 3:7–11

After declaring that Jesus is uniquely superior to the angels (Hebrews 1:5–14) and Moses (Hebrews 3:1–6), the writer issues his second warning in this passage (see Day 3 for the first). The writer quotes Psalm 95:7–11, which cautions Jews against following the example of their forefathers who hardened their hearts against God. In the Septuagint, the word "rebellion" is connected with the name Meribah ("quarrelling") and "testing" with the name Massah (see footnotes in Psalm 95:8 NIV). The Israelites complained against Moses because of water shortages, and almost stoned him. They failed to trust God and His promises even though He had miraculously provided heavenly manna in the desert. Moses named the place Massah and Meribah after the two incidents that occurred there (Exodus 17:1–7; Numbers 20:1–13).

The desert was a place of testing, where one's faith was examined and proven (see Luke 4:1). The Israelites failed miserably; instead of faith, they were filled with unbelief. Instead of praise, their lips produced complaints and murmurings. At the desert, the Israelites had tested God as self-appointed "judges over God"[12] (see Exodus 17:7; Psalm 95:9; Hebrews 3:9). They "tested and tried" (Hebrews 3:9) God's patience and demanded that God prove himself. For 40 years, He showed himself to them; yet they grew in disbelief and disobedience. They had tested God repeatedly (Numbers 14:22) so much so that God was "angry with that generation" (Hebrews 3:10) and declared, "They shall never enter my rest" (v. 11; see Psalm 95:11). The "rest" referred to life in the Promised Land; more distantly, as the writer later explains, it also points to the new life in Christ. The whole Exodus generation died in the desert except for Joshua and Caleb, who had undying faith in God (Numbers 14:23–24, 30).

The lesson from history serves as a stern reminder to the Jewish readers of the epistle—and to us today. We should not harden our hearts (Hebrews 3:7–8). Every time we refuse to respond to God's voice speaking to us, we harden our hearts. The more we do so, the harder they become. Eventually, our hearts will go astray (v. 10) and we begin to drift away dangerously (see Hebrews 2:1).

[12] Hughes, *A Commentary on the Epistle to the Hebrews*, 143.

The Israelites hardened their hearts when they repeatedly failed to trust God and worship Him. Examine your own heart to see whether it is like stone or like flesh (Ezekiel 36:26).

"Their hearts are always going astray" (Hebrews 3:10). How does one make sure that his or her heart remains in Christ (see John 15:7)?

Day 9

Read Hebrews 3:12–19

The writer continues the themes of the earlier passage. He appeals to his readers to respond in faith and to remain with Christ. Persecution was tempting them to leave their Christian faith and return to Judaism. To do so was to repeat the same serious offence committed by their forefathers in the desert. We modern readers can also be tempted to turn away from Christ in favour of old priorities and sinful habits. The writer warns us to stay with Christ and "hold our original conviction firmly to the very end" (Hebrews 3:14; see Matthew 10:22; 24:13).

The "sinful, unbelieving heart" habitually "turns away from the living God" (Hebrews 3:12). We have to be on our guard and "encourage one another daily" (v.13) to remain faithful to Christ. Experiences and victories of the past are important, but each day presents fresh challenges and opportunities for us to show our allegiance to Christ. The present is always "today" (v. 13, used eight times in Hebrews), and we must constantly guard our hearts, faith, and relationship with Christ by trusting and obeying Him.

All those Moses led out of Egypt (except for Joshua and Caleb) perished in the desert. Their "bodies perished in the wilderness" (Hebrews 3:17); with "an average of almost ninety deaths a day".[13] It was a dreadful story of unbelief and disobedience, and its consequences. "Now these things occurred as examples to keep us from setting our hearts on evil things as they did," Paul appealed similarly to his readers (1 Corinthians 10:6). Even we today should not presume that external religious acts and membership in the church guarantee our salvation. What goes on inside us is far more important and determines whether we are really saved or not. We should be responsive to God in Christ and remain so.

Sin is deceitful (Hebrews 3:13) and if we give in to it repeatedly, we harden ourselves to God's grace and salvation. Sin "attacks the individual"[14]—thus every person must examine his or her own faith. Sin and unbelief lock people away from God's Promised Land (His salvation in His eternal kingdom; v. 19). Dealing with sin opens the door to God's blessings.

[13] Stedman, *Hebrews*, 52.

[14] Simon J. Kistemaker, *Exposition of the Epistle to the Hebrews* (Grand Rapids: Baker, 1984), 95.

ThinkThrough

How can we keep our faith fresh such that we are found faithful and true to the Lord Jesus each moment and day? Is there anything tempting you to turn away from Christ? Pray to the Lord for guidance and strength.

Unbelief locks the door to God's salvation and blessings. How is unbelief related to disobedience (Hebrews 3:18–19)? What implication does this have for your present circumstances?

Day 10

Read Hebrews 4:1–11

The Israelites of the Exodus failed to reach the Promised Land; only their offspring did, along with Joshua and Caleb. Two reasons are given for their failure. First, they did not respond in faith to what God told them (Hebrews 4:2). To hear God's Word is one thing; to accept it by faith is another. Second, they did not obey God (v. 6). **Faith and obedience go together; there is no point in claiming to have faith when it is not demonstrated through obedient actions (James 2:18, 26).** Paul writes, "The only thing that counts is faith expressing itself through love" (Galatians 5:6). Jesus connects this love with obedience (John 14:15, 21, 23), for true obedience is always rooted in love for God and neighbours. Because of their lack of believing faith and loving obedience, the Exodus generation did not enter God's rest in the Promised Land.

This lesson has continuing relevance for readers. "The promise of entering his rest still stands" (Hebrews 4:1). The rest that God promises has spiritual significance; it is "a Sabbath-rest for the people of God" (v. 9). It is connected with our salvation in Christ and echoes God's rest on the seventh day after His creation of the universe (v. 4). To enter God's rest is then theologically applied to resting from our own work (v. 10). The gospel of Christ offers us salvation and rest because we are saved not on our own merits but on those of Christ. Just as God completed His work of creation in six days, Christ has also done all that was necessary to save us, declaring, "It is finished" on the cross (John 19:30). All that is required of us is to trust Christ by turning to Him for our salvation. When we do so, we will find our rest (see Matthew 11:28–30).

It is easy to lose our rest—when we turn back from Christ to our former way of life. We will never find spiritual rest outside Christ. The terms "none of you" (Hebrews 4:1) and "no one" (v. 11) express the hope that all who hear will respond with faith and obedience. "Make every effort" (v. 11) suggests that sincerity and commitment are important; we must look for the perfect rest which is the culmination of the rest we begin to experience after placing our faith in Christ. It is serious business.

How can we respond in faith to what we hear? How can we fail to do so? What is God saying to you today?

We are saved by faith in Christ, but why is obedience important to demonstrate that we have faith? How can a Christian "make every effort" (Hebrews 4:11) to enter the rest that is found in Christ?

Day 11

Read Hebrews 4:12–13

God speaks through His Word. How do we ensure that we do not respond to His Word with unbelief and disobedience? The answer is to have a proper view of the nature and power of God's Word. It is not a dead piece of literature, but "alive and active" (Hebrews 4:12). **When we read Scripture, we must recognise that Scripture also reads us.** It is "sharper than any double-edged sword", able to penetrate to the deepest part of us, "dividing soul and spirit, joints and marrow" (v. 12). Picture what happens when your doctor sends you for an MRI or PET scan. The complex machinery uses invisible rays to penetrate your body and return deep and clear images of what lies inside you. The doctor is then able to "see" inside your body and come to a proper diagnosis. In the same way, Scripture probes us deeply to examine our "thoughts and attitudes of the heart" (v. 12).

Nothing can be hidden from the eyes of God, our heavenly Physician. "Everything is uncovered and laid bare before the eyes of him to whom we must give account" (Hebrews 4:13). The phrase "laid bare" is a translation of the Greek *tetrachēlismenos*, a technical word that comes from gladiatorial contests in the ancient Roman world. When a gladiator falls to the ground and is unable to rise, his victorious opponent will grab hold of his hair and pull his head backwards, thus exposing his neck and his trachea (note the word hidden in the Greek term) or windpipe.[15] He will then raise his sword over the neck of his fallen opponent and look to the emperor in the grandstand for instructions. According to popular depictions, if it was thumbs up, the loser was spared. If it was thumbs down, the sword came down on the poor man's neck.

The author uses a similar idea to convey the idea that when reading Scripture we stand exposed to the judgment of God. The difference is that what is raised above us is not a gladiator's sword that kills but a surgeon's scalpel that heals. If we respond to God's Word with fear and trembling (Psalm 119:161), we are saved and healed. If not, we will have to face God in a future day for our failure to believe and obey (John 12:48).

[15] Hughes, *A Commentary on the Epistle to the Hebrews*, 167.

In what way has the Bible been "living and active" in your life? Why do Christians ignore or read the Bible superficially (see James 1:22–25)?

How do we avoid hiding from God and letting the Word expose our true condition? When this happens, what should we do?

Day 12

Read Hebrews 4:14–16

Like Adam and Eve after they had sinned, all human beings stand exposed before God. Instead of running away and hiding from Him in shame, we can make a better response. We can approach His "throne of grace with confidence" (Hebrews 4:16), simply because of what Jesus has accomplished for us. Jesus is thus the "great high priest who has ascended into heaven" (v. 14). There He continues His high priestly ministry by representing us before God the Father. He is our Advocate (1 John 2:1), occupying the most privileged seat in heaven, at the right hand of the Father, and interceding for us (Romans 8:34; Hebrews 7:25). It is astounding that the Son of God (Hebrews 4:14) is our Advocate and Intercessor!

Not only do we have the best ever High Priest, He also has perfect empathy towards us.

He is able to "to feel sympathy for our weaknesses" (Hebrews 4:15) because He was tempted in every way—and was yet without sin. His endurance was "more . . . than ordinary human suffering", simply because He never sinned even though He was fully tempted.[16] Those who give in to temptation (most of us) do not know what it takes to endure fully. Only the sinless "can experience the full intensity of temptation".[17] When we appeal to Him in our suffering and trials, He looks at us with understanding eyes, and we can know that His heart is with us.

It is for this reason that His throne is where we "receive mercy" and "find grace" (Hebrews 4:16). The Jewish readers of this passage would have remembered the mercy seat (on the ark of the covenant) in the old tabernacle, where God met with their sinful forebears through the blood of sacrifice that was sprinkled on it (Exodus 25:21–22). Now, through the sacrifice of Jesus, we can also approach God's mercy seat in heaven to receive mercy (not receiving the punishment that we deserve) and grace (receiving blessings we do not deserve). We are urged to "hold firmly" to this faith centred in Christ (Hebrews 4:14).

[16] Bruce, *Epistle to the Hebrews*, 86.
[17] Stedman, *Hebrews*, 62.

ThinkThrough

We have in Jesus the best High Priest, one who has the highest seat in heaven, has empathy for us, and offers mercy and grace. Think about what this means for you and turn it into prayer.

Is there any struggle in your life that you are facing alone, unable to obtain understanding and empathy from others? Bring it to Jesus, your High Priest, Advocate, Intercessor, and Friend.

Day 13

Read Hebrews 5:1–4

Hebrews contributes significantly to the doctrine that Jesus is our unique and incomparable High Priest. Thus far, the author has argued for the vast superiority of Jesus over the angels and over Moses. Now he shows why Jesus is superior to Aaron the first high priest. He continues his previous argument that Jesus is the very best of high priests.

Aaron, Moses' brother, was chosen by God from among his people to be the first high priest (Exodus 28:1–2; Leviticus 8). The people looked to the high priest to "represent [them] in matters related to God, to offer gifts and sacrifices for sins" (Hebrews 5:1). **The high priest stood between his God and his people, not on his own merits, but on the basis of the blood that was sacrificed in atonement of sins.** Like Aaron, Jesus too was called by God to the office of high priest (v. 4).

The high priest could not just walk confidently into God's presence, for he himself was a sinner ("he himself is subject to weakness", Hebrews 5:2). Thus, he had to offer sacrifices not only for the sins of the people, but for his own (v. 3; see Leviticus 16:6). He was allowed to enter the Holy of Holies, the holiest place in the tabernacle (later, the temple) and only once a year (Hebrews 9:6–7; see Leviticus 16). No one else was allowed to enter this place, where the ark of the covenant was placed. Even Aaron was only given permission to enter on the stipulated day; otherwise he would die (Leviticus 16:2). Tradition has it that the high priest's feet were tied to a rope as he entered the Holy of Holies; in case he died inside because of his sin, his body could be pulled out.

Because the high priest was also a sinner like the people he represented before God, he would be able to deal gently with "those who are ignorant and are going astray" (Hebrews 5:2), unless it got to his head that he was spiritually superior to his people. The author is setting the stage for further discussions that are to follow—that Jesus is our High Priest, who is superior to all the high priests who had preceded Him, and that He would also be gentle to those who are drifting away. The theme of drifting is repeated in Hebrews, urging readers to make sure they do not drift but stay with Jesus, no matter what.

ThinkThrough

Reflect on God's instructions regarding the office of the high priest. What do they say about the nature and holiness of God, and of our true condition in His sight? In what ways might Christians have taken the holiness of God too lightly today?

God calls people to serve Him in various ways. What might God be calling you to do today? How are you living up to that calling?

Day 14

Read Hebrews 5:5–10

The author goes on to show why and how Jesus has become our High Priest. In agreement with the earlier statement that the high priest must be called by God, the writer quotes Psalm 2:7 and 110:4 to show that Jesus was called by God the Father to the office of high priest. God called Him to be His Son and a "priest for ever, in the order of Melchizedek" (Hebrews 5:6). The "indescribable majesty" of the appointment should not escape our notice.[18] More will be said later about Melchizedek, but for now, we can see how Jesus fulfils all the qualifications needed to be a high priest. He was chosen from among men (v. 1)—and that is why He had to be born into the human race, even though He is the Son of God ("the days of Jesus' life on earth", v. 7). On our behalf, he practised "reverent submission" (v. 7). He obeyed the Father in every way and "learned obedience from what he suffered" (v. 8). He identified himself fully with us who are sinful, except that though He was tempted like us, He never sinned (Hebrews 4:15).

Jesus offered up deeply anguished prayers at the Garden of Gethsemane (Mark 14:33–34); His "sweat was like drops of blood falling to the ground" (Luke 22:44). Though He faced the unimaginable agony of the cross where He would be sacrificed, He submitted to the Father's will. The "cries" (kraugē, Hebrews 5:7) that came from His heart were "wrung from him".[19] His reverent submission made Him "perfect" (v. 9), not that He became more sinless or holier, but in the sense that He became the perfect candidate for the office of high priest,[20] in offering himself "as a perfect sacrifice for our sins" (Hebrews 9:14 NLT).

Thus, Jesus became "the source of eternal salvation for all who obey him" (Hebrews 5:9). **The Jewish high priests had to offer annual sacrifices on the Day of Atonement, but Jesus brings a salvation that is good both for now and forever.** The implication for the original readers is that it would be foolish to leave the perfect High Priest for others who cannot deliver. The same lesson applies today. We do ourselves eternal harm when we turn away from Jesus to follow false saviours.

[18] Gooding, An Unshakeable Kingdom, 119.
[19] Barclay, "The Letter to the Hebrews", 47.
[20] Bruce, Epistle to the Hebrews, 52.

What does it mean to have Jesus the Son of God as your High Priest? How can we learn to be more like Him in "reverent submission" (Hebrews 5:7)?

Jesus provides "eternal salvation" (Hebrews 5:9). Reflect on this phrase and seek to understand what it means. Why does the writer say that this is for "all who obey him" (v. 9; see Matthew 7:21; 28:20)? Turn your thoughts into prayer and worship.

Day 15

Read Hebrews 5:11–14

As the author begins to develop the key idea of the Melchizedek priesthood of Jesus, he takes a detour to address the immaturity of his readers, who may have difficulty understanding what he was trying to say. He tells them what they should be and what can be done to achieve that (Hebrews 5:14; see 6:1–3).

There was "much to say about this" (Hebrews 5:11) since the Christian faith has breadth and depth that is seldom appreciated by Christians. The writer says that "it is hard to explain" because his readers have "become dull of hearing" (v. 11 ESV). The word "dull" (Greek *nōthros*) means "slow-moving in mind, torpid in understanding, dull of hearing, witlessly forgetful".[21]

It is understandable that beginners often have difficulty understanding something that is quite new to them. But the writer's complaint is that the readers had remained in elementary school (so to speak) for a long time, and had not grown up to maturity and deeper understanding of God's Word and ways. They should have developed enough to be able to teach others, but instead they still need to be taught the basic stuff—the "elementary truths of God's word"—again and again (Hebrews 5:12). They are compared to infants, who need milk and do not take solid food well (v. 12). Infants need to be weaned off milk at a certain age, when solid food is introduced to their diet. But imagine a teenager still drinking milk like an infant! That is the source of the writer's exasperation over the spiritual development of his readers. They needed to take in solid teaching about righteous living (v. 13), but are unwilling or unable.

Solid food is for the physically mature; likewise, the deeper teachings from God's Word are for the spiritually mature.

Christians become mature by "constant use" of God's Word (Hebrews 5:14)— that is to say, they have constantly read, meditated on, and applied Scripture in their lives through faithful obedience. Understand and applying God's Word in our lives is how we train ourselves to "distinguish good from evil" (v. 14). The Christian is filled with deepening knowledge of God by reading the Bible, developing a biblical mind-set that will help him to discern all that comes his way.

[21] Barclay, "The Letter to the Hebrews", 49.

Why do many
Christians refuse to
grow up? What does
it mean to be mature
in Christ? Compare
yourself now to three
years ago. How
have you matured or
grown in the Lord?

How can a Christian
make "constant
use" (Hebrews 5:14)
of what the Holy
Spirit teaches from
the Word? Why
is understanding
and application so
important in the
maturing process?
Is there any area
where you need to
train yourself in this
regard?

Day 16

Read Hebrews 6:1–3

Imagine having to teach a class of students the alphabet or the multiplication table every year because they are not able to go beyond these lessons. The teacher expects the students to make progress so that more things can be taught. The author, having confronted his readers about their lack of spiritual growth and maturity, now spells out ("therefore", Hebrews 6:1) the basics beyond which they should be going, if they are to mature as Christians. This "basic Christianity" list has six items that can be divided into two sections.

The first section includes "repentance from acts that lead to death" and "faith in God" (Hebrews 6:1). These truths are how one becomes a Christian. Christ and His apostles' initial preaching reflected this when they urged, "Repent and believe" (Mark 1:15; Acts 3:19; 20:21). The phrase "acts that lead to death" refers to "useless rituals" (see footnote in Hebrews 6:1 NIV); the "lifeless moral code" is Judaism without Christ.[22] Repentance must be accompanied by faith in Christ, a turning to Him for salvation (see 1 Thessalonians 1:9). This is how one begins his Christian journey. But there is more to it than that.

The second section has four items: two to do with the beginning of the Christian life and two with its end on earth. "Baptisms" (see footnote in Hebrews 6:2 NIV), probably refers to teachings on ablutions or washings.[23] Baptism is how we are initiated into the faith and incorporated into the church, the body of Christ. Jesus commanded His disciples to make other disciples (Matthew 28:18–20) by baptising them (and then teaching them to obey everything that He has commanded). The laying on of hands was practised on a few occasions in the early church for imparting the Holy Spirit (Acts 8:17)—a practice still done at baptism in some denominations, for healing (Acts 28:8; Mark 16:18), and for ordaining or commissioning (Acts 6:6; 13:3). The next two items have to do with the end of the Christian journey on earth. The resurrection of the body is a basic Christian belief without which our ministry and faith are futile (1 Corinthians 15:14, 17). The doctrine of "eternal judgment" (Hebrews 6:3) is also essential for us to know that God will address all injustices and will bring in a new heaven and earth. **These are all basic doctrines which are not to be discarded, but to be the foundation on which other Christian teachings can be built.**

[22] R. V. Tasker, quoted in Bruce, *Epistle to the Hebrews*, 69.
[23] Bruce, *Epistle to the Hebrews*, 114.

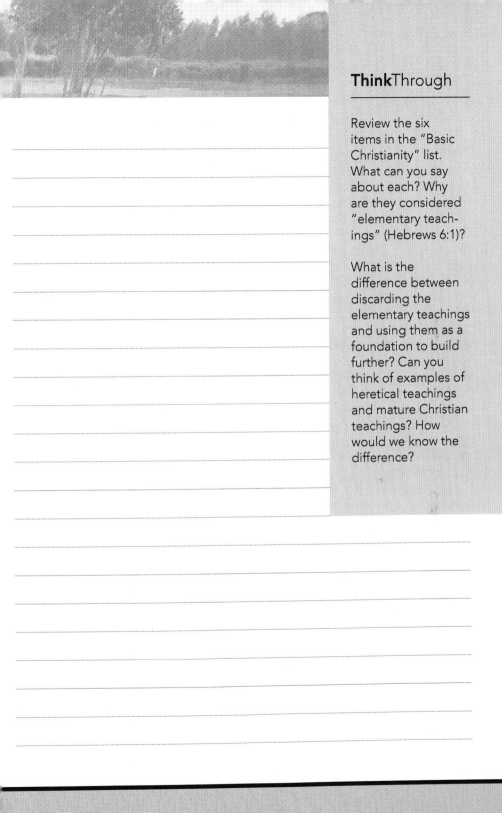

ThinkThrough

Review the six items in the "Basic Christianity" list. What can you say about each? Why are they considered "elementary teachings" (Hebrews 6:1)?

What is the difference between discarding the elementary teachings and using them as a foundation to build further? Can you think of examples of heretical teachings and mature Christian teachings? How would we know the difference?

Day 17

Read Hebrews 6:4–8

This passage contains the third warning in the book (the first two are found on Days 3 and 8). It poses some theological questions and has been the subject of much debate with regard to its proper interpretation. There are those who emphasise that once one is saved by divine choice, one cannot fall into apostasy (abandoning the faith), even though one may fall into sin from time to time. Those who are apostates did not have an authentic experience of the things mentioned in verses 4 to 5. There are others who take the list of Christian experiences and argue that one could still fall into apostasy if one is careless and disobedient. Then there are those who frame the question differently, not having to do with the ultimate security of the believer but with the present need to fully follow Jesus. What is important here is to take our calling to follow Christ with the utmost seriousness and to make every effort not to drift from Christ.

The Hebrews writer gives a harsh warning about those who have left the Christian faith (Hebrews 6:4-6). He describes them as those who were "once enlightened", meaning they had understood the gospel of Christ, and probably been baptised. They had "tasted the heavenly gift" (Hebrews 6:4). This could refer to participation at the Lord's Supper, the heavenly gift being a reference to Christ (John 4:10; 2 Corinthians 9:15). They had "shared in the Holy Spirit" (Hebrews 6:4), probably referring to the new reality of the Holy Spirit in a believer's life. They had "tasted the goodness of the word of God" (by reading and hearing it taught and preached; v. 5). They had also tasted the "powers of the coming age" (having witnessed the signs, wonders, and miracles performed by Jesus or the apostles, and the transformed lives of many believers; v. 5)—having a "foretaste of eternity".[24]

In spite of all these experiences, if they became apostate there would be no hope for them, because their public rejection would be like crucifying Jesus "all over again and subjecting him to public disgrace" (Hebrews 6:6). It would be impossible (v. 4) to bring them back to repentance. The idea is that they would be irredeemably lost. The writer contrasts between a land that produces fruit by drinking the rain that fell on it with another land that only produces thorns and thistles (vv. 7–8). The latter would be cursed and its useless produce burned. **God's grace must not be without effect (1 Corinthians 15:10). It should be evidenced by**

spiritual fruit. This stark warning is meant to shake people out of spiritual slumber before it is too late.

24 Barclay, "The Letter to the Hebrews", 57

How would you apply the disturbing warning in this passage to yourself and to those around you? What do you think is the purpose of the passage?

What does it mean to be like a land that "drinks in the rain often falling on it" (Hebrews 6:7) so that it produces a useful crop? How has God watered your heart, and what sort of fruit has it produced?

Day 18

Read Hebrews 6:9–12

After the harsh warning, the author softens his tone, possibly to show his true purpose for writing. He addresses his readers as "dear friends" (Hebrews 6:9). He assures them, "we are convinced of better things in your case" (v. 9). These better things have to do with true salvation (v. 9). In saying this, the author suggests that he knew that his readers were saved and had an ongoing relationship with Christ. God is not blind and notes all that goes on in our hearts and lives. The author assures his readers that their love for God has not gone unnoticed (v. 10). Note that love for God is proven by Christian love and service, "as you have helped his people and continue to help them" (v. 10). God does not forget such work and will justly reward His people; He is "not unjust" (v. 10). They had been diligent Christians at one time, who had taken their faith seriously.

But the temptations are very real. One can lose one's passion and discipline ("become lazy", Hebrews 6:12). One can lose one's perseverance when prayers seem to be unanswered, when persecution gathers momentum, and when the going gets tough. This was a real challenge for the original readers of Hebrews. Many of them were tempted to give up their Christian faith and identity to escape the growing persecution against the church. It would be easier for them to return to their old Jewish faith. But that would be a disaster, as the author continues to point out to them. They must persevere with "this same diligence" that they had shown "to the very end" (v. 11). This message was for "each of you" (v. 11). There are to be no exceptions, because no one can escape the implications. They must stand firm till the end (Hebrews 3:14; Matthew 24:13). Only by doing so would they make their hope sure (Hebrews 6:11). This hope has to do with what was ahead: the return of Christ, the final judgment, and the life everlasting. It has to do with what we do not yet have (Romans 8:25), a future inheritance that has been promised by God (Hebrews 6:12).

We make sure of this hope by continuing in faith, for "faith is confidence in what we hope for" (Hebrews 11:1). This requires both "faith and patience" (6:12). Faith because it is rooted in one's relationship with and trust in the unseen Christ. Patience because He has His own timetable, and we must wait for Him to act.

ThinkThrough

How does the author encourage his readers? What lessons can we learn in exhorting others?

Reflect on the diligence with which we are to follow Christ. What evidence is there in your life that this is so? What factors tempt you to give up or compromise? What would be the consequences of giving in?

Day 19

Read Hebrews 6:13–20

A great example in the history of the Jews of "faith and patience" (Hebrews 6:12) is Abraham. God called him with a promise of blessing him with numerous descendants (Genesis 12:2). It took 25 years before that promise began to be fulfilled with the birth of Isaac. During the period of waiting, God continued to sustain Abraham's faith with His repeated promises (Genesis 12:7; 17:5–6). Then in Genesis 22:16–18, God made the same promise, this time with an oath. This was after Abraham showed that he trusted God enough to be willing to sacrifice Isaac. The writer argues that God need not make any oath, for one has to swear an oath on "someone greater than themselves" (Hebrews 6:16). Although there is no one greater than God, nevertheless, in accommodating the need of Abraham and his descendants to trust God, God swore an oath—on himself (v.13). This was a double assurance to Abraham. First, God does not lie and His character never changes. Second, the oath was a specific guarantee that what God had promised would come to pass. On these two counts ("unchangeable things", v. 18), we can be greatly encouraged with a "firm and secure" hope (v. 19) that God will bestow His promised blessings if we persevere in our faith.

This hope is rooted in Christ, who is the ultimate fruit of God's promise to Abraham—that he will be blessed with many descendants. God reaffirmed His promise to Abraham after Isaac was born (Genesis 22:16–18). Abraham even lived to see the next stage of God's promise realised when Esau and Jacob were born (Genesis 25:23; see 25:7, 26). God's promise was fully expressed in Christ, through whom Abraham's innumerable descendants (Galatians 6:16; the Israel of faith, the church) would be blessed. This is a sure hope, "an anchor for the soul" (Hebrews 6:19). The anchor was one of the earliest symbols of the Christian faith; the Greek word *anchura* also sounded like *en kurio* ("in Christ", a repeated phrase in the New Testament).

This anchor of hope is connected with Jesus our *prodromos* ("our official forerunner", who went before us),[25] who as our unique High Priest entered beyond the curtain to the Holy of Holies, so that the way can be made safe for us. In this regard, His priesthood is of the "order of Melchizedek" (Hebrews 5:6), the significance of which will be explained later. **In Christ, God's ancient promise has been fulfilled, and our hearts can be firmly encouraged to continue keeping the faith.**

[25] Gooding, *An Unshakeable Kingdom*, 115.

Consider Abraham's example. Reflect on how God sought to sustain his faith, and how he waited for it to be fulfilled. What lessons can you draw from this in your own life?

Jesus is our forerunner. What does this mean for you personally? Thank Him today!

Day 20

Read Hebrews 7:1–3

The Jews have known no priesthood other than the Aaronic one, but now the writer of Hebrews tells his readers that there is yet a higher order of priesthood, one to which Jesus belongs.

This passage (in the central chapter of Hebrews)[26] reveals more about the mysterious Melchizedek (Genesis 14:18–20). He was both the king of Salem (Jerusalem) and a "priest of God Most High" (Hebrews 7:1). As priest, he brought out bread and wine and blessed Abraham, the forefather of the Jews (and all the people of faith). Abraham then gave Melchizedek a tithe (tenth) of everything. Hebrews introduces this ancient Melchizedek as a mysterious figure who helps us to understand who Christ is: one who is both priest and king. His name means "king of righteousness" (v. 2)—a unique term, which reminds us of Christ. He was also known as the "king of Salem", meaning "king of peace" (v. 2). These terms are used by the author to show that he was not an ordinary priest and king. He was an extraordinary person.

This is reiterated further in verse 3. Melchizedek is a stranger who blazes onto the scene. No one knows who his parents were. Unlike the Levitical priesthood, who had to prove their ancestry, he is "without genealogy" (no background or pedigree). He is "without beginning of days or end of life". No one knows when he was born or when he died, there being no such record. This suggests that he, symbolically, lives for ever, as a type of Christ,[27] and that his priesthood is one that lasts for ever.

This idea that the priesthood of Jesus is similar to or the same as that of Melchizedek is a central idea in Hebrews. First, we have Hebrews 5:6 where God is depicted as saying to Christ, "You are a priest for ever, in the order of Melchizedek". Then in Hebrews 6:20, it is declared that as our forerunner who entered the Holy of Holies, Jesus "has become a high priest for ever, in the order of Melchizedek". Then this is further explained in Hebrews 7. The question is asked whether Melchizedek was in fact the pre-incarnate Christ, as some commentators think. But that was most likely not the case, for though he seems to be a mysterious figure, he is referred to as "*resembling* the Son of God" (Hebrews 7:3) rather than "the Son of God". Although he was only a human being, the lack of details about his life makes him the perfect "facsimile (type) of which Christ is the reality".[28]

[26] Thomas, *Hebrews*, 81.
[27] Hughes, *A Commentary on the Epistle to the Hebrews*, 248.
[28] G. C. D. Howley, ed., *A New Testament Commentary* (Grand Rapids: Zondervan, 1969), 552.

ThinkThrough

Why do you think the author takes pains to show that the priesthood of Jesus is unique, and that it can be compared to the mysterious priest and king who met Abraham? Does this mean anything to us today?

In what ways does Jesus remain a mystery to you? What happens when we think we know everything about Him?

Day 21

Read Hebrews 7:4–10

The author urges his readers to "just think how great [Melchizedek] was" (Hebrews 7:4). He notes the amazing picture, recorded in Genesis, of patriarch Abraham tithing to this mysterious priest-king. Abraham had just rescued Lot and the other inhabitants of Sodom who had been taken captive by a coalition of local kings. Abraham gave Melchizedek "a tenth of the plunder" (v. 4). According to the law, Israelites were to give a tithe to the priests who had descended from the tribe of Levi (v. 5; Numbers 18:21, 26). But Melchizedek was not a Levite, or even an Israelite. In fact, he appeared even before Levi, 430 years before the law was given through Moses (Exodus 12:40; Galatians 3:17). Why would Abraham present him with a tithe when he was a stranger?

By referring to this historical event, the writer shows that Melchizedek was one who was greater than Abraham. It was Melchizedek who blessed Abraham, not the other way around. "And without doubt the lesser is blessed by the greater" (Hebrews 7:7). The writer further pushes home his point by differentiating the tithe received by the Levitical priesthood of the Jews and that received by Melchizedek from Abraham. The Levitical priests are "people who die" while Melchizedek "is declared to be living" (v. 8; see Hebrews 5:6; 6:20). Using typical rabbinic ways of interpreting Scripture (in other words, sometimes going beyond the literal and finding symbolic or allegorical meaning),[29] the author indicates that when Abraham paid the tithe to Melchizedek, we could say that Levi, who was not yet born but in some way existed potentially in Abraham, participated in that tithe-giving. Levi and his descendants, who collected their rightful tithes from Israel, had in fact already given their tithe to Melchizedek through Abraham their forefather (7:9–10).

The argument here is that the priesthood of Melchizedek is superior to that of the Levitical one. All this is designed to make the Jewish Christians, who were the original readers, pay attention to the uniqueness of Christ. **Christ was their High Priest like no other high priest before Him.** By declaring that the priesthood of Christ is of the order of Melchizedek, the author uses this mysterious character from the past to shed light on Christ and His unique ministry and office. It urges us to pay closer attention to Jesus.

[29] Barclay, "The Letter to the Hebrews", 67–68.

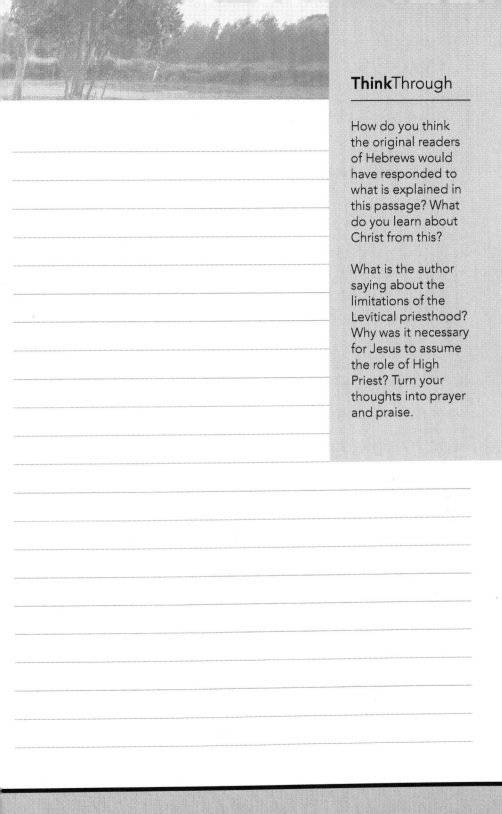

ThinkThrough

How do you think the original readers of Hebrews would have responded to what is explained in this passage? What do you learn about Christ from this?

What is the author saying about the limitations of the Levitical priesthood? Why was it necessary for Jesus to assume the role of High Priest? Turn your thoughts into prayer and praise.

Day 22

Read Hebrews 7:11–14

The author relentlessly emphasises the uniqueness of Jesus as our High Priest, far above all the priests and high priests who had served in the religion of Israel as constituted by the law of Moses. He argues that the Levitical priesthood, useful as it was in the worship of Israel, was nevertheless insufficient. It was not perfect. "If perfection could have been attained through the Levitical priesthood . . . why was there still need for another priest to come" (Hebrews 7:11). **The priesthood of Jesus was necessary to provide a perfect priest for Israel and the world.** Jesus does not belong to the order of Aaron, for He did not come in that hereditary line of priests. Instead He comes from the order of Melchizedek (v. 11).

Jesus belonged to the tribe of Judah (Hebrews 7:14). No priests had come from that tribe (v. 13), though kings, starting from David, had come from that royal line. But like Melchizedek, who was both king and priest, Jesus too was both king and priest—the perfect King and Priest. The priestly ministry of Jesus was prefigured by the mysterious king-priest Melchizedek. So it was really before Jesus, the perfect King-Priest, that Abraham (and through him Levi and all the Levitical priests) submitted. The reality is that Jesus introduces a new eternal priesthood centred in Him.

This would have answered anyone having trouble accepting the priesthood of Jesus, since He was not a descendent of Aaron. The writer shows that Jesus' priestly ministry was valid because it belonged to a different order. In fact, for this reason, it is superior to the priestly ministry of the Aaronic priests of Israel.

With the eternal priesthood of Jesus in place, the old Levitical priesthood was no longer necessary (Hebrews 7:12), having been superseded by the Melchizedek priesthood of Jesus. Accordingly, the old Mosaic law which supported the Levitical priesthood, offering divine forgiveness to repentant Israelites through the sacrificial system, is no longer necessary too. The old priesthood and the law were not able to bring about perfection. Instead they foreshadowed the coming of Christ, who alone as the perfect High Priest and the Lord of the New Covenant could bring about perfection. "The Melchizedek priesthood of Jesus was in the mind of God centuries before the Levitical priesthood and the law".[30] The law and the priesthood were temporary "shadows" of the reality which is Christ, whose high priestly office has "cosmic significance".[31]

[30] Stedman, *Hebrews*, 83.
[31] Gooding, *An Unshakeable Kingdom*, 119.

In what ways could Christians grow to rely on methods of worship and spiritual growth apart from Jesus? How can we ensure that we rely on Christ's perfect ministry for our daily as well as ultimate needs?

Why is Jesus both a Priest and a King, and what importance does this have for the way He ministers to you? How would you therefore respond to Him?

Day 23

Read Hebrews 7:15–19

A Levitical priest is put in place only if he can prove his ancestry from Levi (Nehemiah 7:63–65). When he died, another Levite would take his place. The Melchizedek priesthood is not based on hereditary lineage, but "on the basis of the power of an indestructible life" (Hebrews 7:16). Jesus will not die, for death has no hold on Him. We have already seen how Melchizedek is mysteriously described as "without beginning of days or end of life" (v. 3). It is not likely that Melchizedek was an immortal person (or that he was the pre-incarnate Christ) but the lack of details about his pedigree or how long he lived is used by the writer to present him as a type for Jesus, the eternal priest (see Day 20). Therefore, Jesus is our eternal Priest, whose lineage does not belong to the Levitical priests, but whose priesthood arises from his role as the eternal Davidic Priest-King and Son of God, who fulfils all the prophecies made about Him. For the fourth time, Psalm 110:4 is used to show that Jesus is a priest for ever, "in the order of Melchizedek" (v. 17). Through His glorious resurrection, Jesus proved that His life cannot be ended, and that it is indestructible. Thus, His priesthood is for ever.

Accordingly, the "former regulation" (the law and the Levitical priesthood) is "set aside" (*athetēsis*, meaning "cancelled") because it is "weak and useless", unable to save us from our sins (Hebrews 7:18). The reason is that "the law made nothing perfect"—its role being limited to pointing out our need for Christ, who is the "better hope" who draws us effectively near to God (v. 19; see Hebrews 10:22). The Levitical priesthood is not effective because it "cannot cleanse from sin or provide power to obey".[32] **There is no priest like Jesus who can wash away our sins and give us life eternal.** "Through his unique sacrifice he fulfilled the responsibilities of the Aaronic priesthood, and through his endless life he assumes the priesthood in the order of Melchizedek."[33] He is the unique and best priest we can find in history.

In Jesus, we find our eternal priest, one we can rely on for ever to give us access to God by cleansing us and providing power to do the will of God. We should recognise who He is, and trust and worship Him all our days.

[32] Stedman, *Hebrews*, 84.
[33] Kistemaker, *Exposition of the Epistle to the Hebrews*, 146.

Why are the old priesthood and law seen as weak and useless? What popular "saviours" and "priests" might we be tempted to turn to for salvation?

How does Jesus help us to draw near to God? How have you experienced this?

Day 24

Read Hebrews 7:20–22

Psalm 110:4 is the key text that the author of Hebrews uses repeatedly to assure us of the eternal priesthood of Jesus. This time he emphasises that the priesthood of Jesus came with a divine oath. "The Lord has sworn and will not change his mind: 'You are a priest for ever'" (Hebrews 7:21). We saw in Hebrews 6:17 how God made an oath with regard to Abraham's descendants. That promise was eventually fulfilled in Christ, who more than Abraham could have imagined, made it possible for the spiritual offspring of Abraham to multiply into a vast number. This promise that God made to Abraham is connected with Jesus "[becoming] a high priest for ever, in the order of Melchizedek" (6:20).

This Melchizedek priesthood of Jesus is a certainty (Psalm 110:4). God has sworn it and will not change His mind about it; there is no other alternative and no other plan. **Jesus is the High Priest for ever, and that will never change. Because of this divine oath, Jesus "has become the guarantor of a better covenant" (Hebrews 7:22).** The Greek word *enguos* ("guarantor", used only here in the New Testament) means "surety", one "who guarantees that some undertaking will be honoured".[34] The "better covenant" refers to the new covenant that Jesus established. At the Last Supper with His disciples, Jesus said, "This cup is the new covenant in my blood, which is poured out for you" (Luke 22:20). This new covenant replaces the old covenant that is based on the law of Moses and the temple sacrificial rituals performed by the Levitical priests. Now that Jesus has come, the old covenant is superseded by the new covenant, which is based on the once-for-all sacrifice of Jesus. In this new covenant, God offers us salvation freely in His grace.

We can imagine how this must have appealed to the Jewish Christians who were tempted, for various reasons, to leave the Christian faith to return to their Jewish faith. Why return to something that has already become redundant? Why leave the eternal solution from heaven for something that was only temporary? The Christian must remain with Christ who himself is the guarantee of the effectiveness of His new covenant.

[34] Barclay, "The Letter to the Hebrews", 81.

The ministry of Jesus comes with God's oath (Hebrews 7:21) and Jesus' own guarantee (v. 22). What does this mean for you? How can you thank God for such a profound assurance? How does it help when you face doubts and difficulties?

How does Jesus, our eternal priest and surety, assure you of His constant presence and ministry? If you have any difficulty in experiencing this, tell Jesus about it in prayer.

Day 25

Read Hebrews 7:23–25

Suppose you appeal to a high official about a personal problem which others are unable or unwilling to help resolve. You are relieved when this wise and compassionate official agrees to help. But what would happen if he were to suddenly die? You would have lost your patron and advocate. You would return to your original helpless situation. This passage reminds readers that the old Levitical priesthood had to do with a continuous stream of mortal priests who, like the hymn "O God, Our Help in Ages Past" (sixth and seventh stanzas) says, are taken away by time, one after the other. No one priest had continued in priestly office beyond his limited lifetime.

But Jesus is absolutely different. **The priesthood of Jesus is superior to any other priesthood because it comes with a divine guarantee and oath.** Secondly, it is a "permanent priesthood" (Hebrews 7:24). He died— yes, for our sins, and He rose from the dead; He now lives for ever. He therefore has a permanent priesthood; He is for ever our priest. Whatever He has promised will not be abandoned because He will never die. This has significant results in our lives, for He "is able to save completely those who come to God through him" (Hebrews

7:25). As our High Priest, He "lives to intercede" for us (v. 25) at the Father's right hand (Romans 8:34; Hebrews 8:1). We have some idea of how He does this by examining His High Priestly Prayer in John 17. The Bible says that He is our Advocate in heaven, appealing on our behalf. His intercession for us is ongoing, having redeemed us from our sins, He, together with the Holy Spirit, will continue to make us grow in Christlikeness (2 Corinthians 3:18). We know that what He has begun will be brought to perfect completion on His day (Philippians 1:6). We know that in Christ we will be presented before God "without fault and with great joy" (Jude 24).

How wonderful it is that we have an eternal Advocate who will never vacate His office. He will be in His priestly office for ever. Whatever He has promised us, He is capable of carrying out fully. We should therefore worship Him with gratitude, knowing that we have an assurance that can never be taken away from us.

ThinkThrough

Reflect on what it means to have a priest who will never die. Tell Jesus how grateful you are that you have found Him (or rather He has found you). Tell Him how much you trust Him to carry out all His promises fully.

What do you think Jesus is saying to the Father about you? What would He be interceding on your behalf about? What does it mean for you that Jesus is praying for you?

Day 26

Read Hebrews 7:26–28

Jesus is the unique, divinely promised priest ordained by God, the eternal priest who will never vacate His office. He has also provided a sacrifice that is far above all the sacrifices offered over the centuries by the Levitical priests: "He sacrificed for their sins once for all" (Hebrews 7:27). He sacrificed himself in atonement for our sins, effectively securing the forgiveness of our sins. The author of Hebrews writes that the sacrifices made by the Levitical priests had to be repeated "day after day" (v. 27) because they did not ultimately remove the problem of sin. Sin became like a chronic medical condition, the symptoms of which had to be kept under control with the daily "treatment" provided by the daily sacrifices at the temple. Many of the people had reduced the sacrifices to a mere ritual. That explains why God in His Word, at times, seems to downplay the importance of the daily sacrifices, because the people failed to see the real work of God in solving the problem of sin. "'The multitude of your sacrifices—what are they to me?' says the LORD. 'I have more than enough of burnt offerings, of rams and the fat of fattened animals; I have no pleasure in the blood of bulls and lambs and goats.'" (Isaiah 1:11). "To obey is better than sacrifice" (1 Samuel 15:22).

All the old priestly sacrifices pointed to the one sacrifice that really matters, that provides a decisive, unique, and truly effective solution to the problem of human sin; "it suffices to eternity".[35] **When Jesus "offered himself" as the perfect sacrifice, He made all other sacrifices redundant and unnecessary.** The Lamb of God was slain for our sins and no other lambs needed to be slain. His sacrifice is the only effective "medicine" and "cure" for our sinful condition. In this way, Jesus is the High Priest who truly "meets our need" (Hebrews 7:26).

He is "holy, blameless, pure, set apart from sinners, exalted above the heavens" (Hebrews 7:26), unlike any of the Levitical priests who had to offer sacrifices for their own sins even as they offered sacrifices for the sins of others (v. 27). These priests were "men in all their weakness", but Jesus the High Priest according to the order of Melchizedek comes with God's oath—and there is no perfect priesthood like His (v. 28).

[35] Hughes, *A Commentary on the Epistle to the Hebrews,* 278.

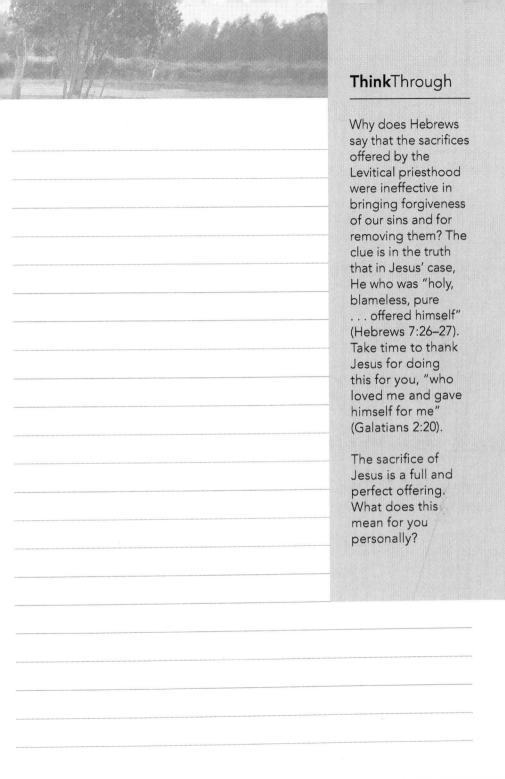

ThinkThrough

Why does Hebrews say that the sacrifices offered by the Levitical priesthood were ineffective in bringing forgiveness of our sins and for removing them? The clue is in the truth that in Jesus' case, He who was "holy, blameless, pure . . . offered himself" (Hebrews 7:26–27). Take time to thank Jesus for doing this for you, "who loved me and gave himself for me" (Galatians 2:20).

The sacrifice of Jesus is a full and perfect offering. What does this mean for you personally?

Day 27

Read Hebrews 8:1–7

The author of Hebrews has thus far been showing how Jesus is superior to the angels, to Moses, and the Levitical priests. Now he continues his argument to show that the ministry of Jesus is superior to that of the Old Testament ministers, whose work in the earthly temple is far surpassed by the ministry of Jesus in the heavenly sanctuary. There is a "true tabernacle" in heaven "set up by the Lord" himself (Hebrews 8:2), in the very presence of God on His throne. Jesus serves as our High Priest in this heavenly tabernacle and what He does there has substantial and eternal consequences for us. He sits at the right hand of the Father, a position of the highest honour, authority, and power (v. 1).

What then about the earthly tabernacle where the Levitical priests went about their ministry? Made according to God's instructions (Exodus 25:9, 40), the earthly tabernacle (and temple) was a "copy and shadow of what is in heaven" (Hebrews 8:5). One is a shadow while the other is the substance; the difference between, say, a photograph and the actual person. **The ministry of Jesus in the heavenly tabernacle is superior to that of the priests in the earthly tabernacle.** One is based on the new covenant (with "better promises", v. 6). The other has already been made redundant. The author's argument is that if there was nothing wrong (or inadequate) with the old covenant, then there would be no need for a new and better one (v. 7). The implication is clear. Who Jesus is (the Son of God), where He is ministering (in the heavenly tabernacle), and what He has done for us (He offered himself as a once for all sacrifice that need not be repeated because of its absolute efficacy) show that there is no one like Jesus—He is our one and only High Priest, in whom God's promises have found full expression.

Normally, outside the Bible, the Greek word *sunthēkē* is used for the idea of covenant—an agreement between two parties, whether it is in a marriage or a pact between two countries. But here a different word is used— *diathēkē*—meaning not an agreement but a will.[36] The new covenant God makes with us in Christ is not an agreement between equals (indeed, neither was the old covenant between God and Abraham), but one made solely by the testator (the author of the will). The other party has no right to change the will, only to accept or reject it. We approach God through Christ on God's terms, never our own.

[36] Barclay, "The Letter to the Hebrews", 91.

ThinkThrough

The writer of Hebrews says that the temple was merely a pale reflection of the heavenly tabernacle (Hebrews 8:5). How would this have persuaded his readers to stay with Christ? How does this persuade you about the ministry of Jesus?

We approach God through Christ on God's terms, never our own. What implications does this have for you?

Day 28

Read Hebrews 8:8–13

The new covenant in Christ is radically different from the old one. The author quotes Jeremiah 31:31–34 to show a few things about it. First, the new covenant should not be a total surprise as God had long foretold that He would make a new covenant with His people (Hebrews 8:8; Jeremiah 31:31–34). Second, the word for new is *kainos* (Hebrews 8:8), meaning it is not only new in terms of the passage of time (for which the word *neos* would have been used, see Hebrews 12:24), but also new in quality.

The disappointing results associated with the old covenant were due to the sinful disobedience of the Israelite forefathers and their failure to be faithful to God according to the terms of the covenant. In the old covenant, the Lord placed His word before the people, and they often chose to reject it. But in the new covenant, God promised to "put my laws in their minds and write them on their hearts" (Hebrews 8:10). The Word would be internalised through the work of the Holy Spirit, of whom Jesus said, "He will guide you into all the truth" (John 16:13; "[God's] word is truth", John 17:17); and "remind you of everything I have said to you" (John 14:26). In the new covenant, Jesus gives the Holy Spirit to His disciples (John 20:22). God not only

expects us to be faithful, but He will also give us the means to do so as we are filled with the Word (Colossians 3:16) and Spirit of Christ (Ephesians 5:18).

The result of such an infilling is that the person will know God and does not need to be taught or told by others; he will experience God first hand. No one will need to know God through the mediation of others, or relate to God by merely following others. Every person will know God, no matter who they are ("from the least of them to the greatest", Hebrews 8:11). In this new covenant, God says "I will be their God, and they will be my people" (v. 10), having forgiven and forgotten their sins on the basis of the work of Christ on the cross (v. 12).

Thus, the old covenant is "obsolete and outdated" and will "soon disappear" (Hebrews 8:13). It is *gēraskōn* (outdated) and about to *aphanismos* (disappear). It would be foolish to hang on to the old after the new has come.

ThinkThrough

The new covenant makes it possible for Christ's Word to dwell within us. What has this meant for you? What could prevent us from being filled with God's Word?

How does the Holy Spirit make a profound difference in the new covenant? What has been your experience of the Holy Spirit in relation to Christ and the Word of God?

Day 29

Read Hebrews 9:1–5

The writer ends chapter 8 by showing how the new covenant in Christ supersedes the old covenant established by the law of Moses. The old covenant was centred on the worship of God in the tabernacle that was constructed according to God's detailed plans. The original readers would have been familiar with the tabernacle story (Exodus 25–31 and 35–40)—the history and furnishing details and how the worship of God was carried out (the "regulations for worship", Hebrews 9:1). The writer does not repeat the details except those that have significance for the point he is making.

The tabernacle, first constructed during the wilderness wanderings under Moses, was an "earthly sanctuary" (Hebrews 9:1). One entered the tabernacle grounds through one gate. This area was called the courtyard and was where all the worshippers would congregate. The tabernacle itself (vv. 2–3) had a first room called the Holy Place, where only priests could enter to do their priestly work. Inside this room were the seven-branched golden lampstand (which was kept burning always), and the table for the consecrated bread (twelve loaves, changed every Sabbath, and eaten only by the priests). There was also the golden altar of incense (described here as being in the Holy of Holies), which is burnt twice daily (morning and evening) to symbolise the prayers of the people. Beyond the Holy Place is the "Most Holy Place" (v. 3), where only the high priest could enter once every year. Inside was the gold covered ark of the covenant, containing a golden jar of manna which was never spoiled (Exodus 16:32), Aaron's staff that had budded to bear fruit when his priesthood was challenged (Numbers 17:8–10), and the stone tablets of the covenant, written by the finger of God (Deuteronomy 10:1–5)—all relating to original events during the Exodus event. The cover of the ark was called the mercy seat (the "atonement cover", Hebrews 9:5). Two golden cherubim (angels) were on the atonement cover covering it. The ark represented God's glorious presence and His covenant with Israel. God promised that He would meet His people in the Holy of Holies (Exodus 25:22).

All this was done according to God's instructions in the law. For centuries it was the prescribed way for sinful people to approach and worship a holy God. But when Christ came, it became redundant, for it was clear that the architecture, furnishings, and practices in the temple were but a shadow of the reality that is in Christ. **Jesus opened a way right into the Holy of Holies for anyone seeking God to enter.**

ThinkThrough

Why do you think God gave detailed instructions about the tabernacle? How can the structure and worship at the tabernacle help us to understand the Person and work of Christ better?

The New Testament teaches that we (individually and corporately) are God's temple (1 Corinthians 3:16; 6:19). What implications are there for us? In Christ, you now have full access to God. Spend a moment to reflect on what this means and worship Christ.

Day 30

Read Hebrews 9:6–10

While the tabernacle (and later the temple) was in place, the regular worship of the people of Israel went on. Everything was constructed and used in an orderly fashion. The people were restricted to the courtyard. The priests who alone could enter the Holy Place went in there to perform their regular priestly duties (Hebrews 9:6)—to attend to the lampstand, the table, and the altar of incense. These were all symbolic of the work of God and His relationship with His people. Only the high priest could enter the Holy of Holies, and only once a year (Leviticus 16; see also Hebrews 9:7)—to emphasise the holiness of God who is unapproachable (Exodus 19:21–24; see 1 Timothy 6:16), such that anyone who sees Him face to face would die (Exodus 33:20). It is for this reason that the high priest could only enter the Holy of Holies after blood had been shed in sacrifice—for his own sins and that of his people (Hebrews 9:7). For "without the shedding of blood there is no forgiveness" (v. 22).

The Jews were familiar with the details of worship in the tabernacle. But it was clear, as Hebrews argues, that all this was not the ultimate reality—only a shadow that points to the reality. The Holy Spirit has shown that "the way into the Most Holy Place had not yet been disclosed as long as the first tabernacle was still functioning" (Hebrews 9:8). In the earthly temple, a curtain veiled the way to the Most Holy Place, and God. When Jesus died, the curtain was torn into two from top to bottom (Matthew 27:51), symbolising how His sacrifice had removed the separation between God and man. The earthly tabernacle and its sacrificial and liturgical system were only a shadow and model ("an illustration" or a "parable")[37] of the present reality found in Christ (Hebrews 9:9).

On their own, the gifts and sacrifices (this phrase is used also in Hebrews 5:1 and 8:8 to refer specifically to gifts and sacrifices which is offered for atonement of sins and to make peace with God; see Leviticus 1–7; 9:7, 15–22) were not able to "clear the conscience of the worshipper (Hebrews 9:9). The guilt for sins still remained in the conscience (the inner awareness of objective guilt)[38] of the sinner (Hebrews 10:11). **Hebrews argues that no amount of temple sacrifices can take away the painful effects of the guilty conscience.** What was done at the tabernacle had only an outward effect, "a matter of food and drink and various ceremonial washings" (Hebrews 9:10). The rituals and practices were confined to "external regulations" (v. 10). They cannot solve the inward needs of people: their guilty conscience and broken relationship with God. A "new order" (v. 10) was needed—which is found in Christ. Praise be to God!

37 Hughes, *A Commentary on the Epistle to the Hebrews*, 324.
38 Mary Healy, *Hebrews* (Grand Rapids: Baker Academic, 2016), 194.

ThinkThrough

Why were the sacrifices in the tabernacle unable to clear the guilty conscience of the sinner? Why is it that trying to save ourselves by living piously cannot improve the situation?

When can religious ritual become an empty act that does not touch the inner realities of the worshipper? How can you worship from the depths of your heart?

Day 31

Read Hebrews 9:11–14

While the old tabernacle system of worship is a type (or a shadow) of the reality found in Christ, we can still learn many lessons from the old patterns. By looking at the old one, we can better understand the new order.

The sacrifice of animals was central to the old order. Blood had to be shed to bring about divine forgiveness and ritual purity. In the new order, blood is also a central reality. Christ has come now as our High Priest and what He does includes the "good things that are now already here" (Hebrews 9:11) as well as what we shall receive in the future through Him. We can experience His reality in the present even as it will be more perfectly seen in the future when He returns. As our unique High Priest, He goes not into the earthly tabernacle, but into the "more perfect tabernacle" (v. 11), making it possible for us to enter God's presence without the need for animal sacrifices (see Ephesians 2:6). Jesus enters the Holy of Holies in a way no other high priest could enter, not with the blood of animals, but His own blood—His own life, for blood is life (see Leviticus 17:11).

His blood is offered "once for all" (Hebrews 9:12), for unlike the old system, His sacrifice need not be repeated. It has permanent and eternally lasting effects in securing our forgiveness and reconciliation with God. In short, through the blood of Christ we have "eternal redemption" (v. 12). **The blood of animals only brought outward ritual purity. It is the blood of Christ the Lamb of God that can cleanse our conscience and bring about true forgiveness and holiness.** By the power of the "eternal Spirit" (v. 14), Jesus offered himself as an unblemished sacrifice to God (note how all persons of the Trinity are involved here). His sacrifice of himself on our behalf is able to "cleanse our consciences" (v. 14).

The blood of Jesus is able to provide not only pardon for our sins by removing our guilt, but also provides power to overcome sins that produce guilty consciences, "from acts that lead to death" (Hebrews 9:14). We are then able to "serve the living God" (v. 14), from hearts that have been made clean and kept clean by the power of Christ and His Spirit.

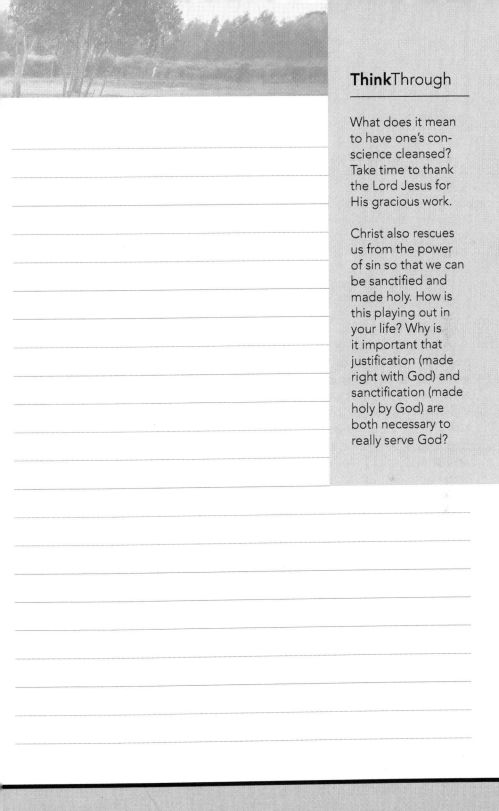

ThinkThrough

What does it mean to have one's conscience cleansed? Take time to thank the Lord Jesus for His gracious work.

Christ also rescues us from the power of sin so that we can be sanctified and made holy. How is this playing out in your life? Why is it important that justification (made right with God) and sanctification (made holy by God) are both necessary to really serve God?

Day 32

Read Hebrews 9:15–22

Jesus shed His blood for our forgiveness and to bring into effect the new covenant. The Greek word used to describe the Hebrew covenant actually refers to a will or testament.[39] A will does not come into effect before the testator (the author of the will) dies (Hebrews 9:16–17). Under the old covenant, animal sacrifices were only a temporary provision of temporary sacrifices till the real, once-and-for-all sacrifice (of the Lamb of God) was made. **In the case of the new covenant, Jesus is *both* the testator and executor of the will—He died for us, and then rose victoriously from the dead to make the new covenant real in our lives.**

Moses, after proclaiming God's law to the people, took the blood of calves and sprinkled the blood on the scroll (containing God's covenant and law) and the people. He referred to the blood as "the blood of the covenant" (Hebrews 9:20; see Exodus 24:8). He also sprinkled the blood on the tabernacle and its contents (Hebrews 9:21). The operating principle is that "without the shedding of blood there is no forgiveness" (v. 22).

This same principle applies to Jesus. It is His blood that purifies us from our sins. "He has died as a ransom to set them free from the sins committed under the first covenant" (Hebrews 9:15). Through His death we receive God's forgiveness and are saved from the punishment for our sins, for He took our place. His death put into effect the new covenant: "This is my blood of the covenant, which is poured out for many for the forgiveness of sins" (Matthew 26:28). But Jesus is also the executor of the will. He rose from the dead and now reigns to bring into effect the blessings of the new covenant into our lives, that we "may receive the promised eternal inheritance" (Hebrews 9:15).

[39] Hughes, *A Commentary on the Epistle to the Hebrews*, 369.

ThinkThrough

How is Christ the "mediator of a new covenant" (Hebrews 9:15)? In what way is He both the testator and executor of the will? How does this apply to your life?

Reflect on the blood of Jesus and what it means to you. How does the death of Christ bring you divine forgiveness and His life mediate for you all of God's rich blessings?

Day 33

Read Hebrews 9:23–28

Jesus (His Person, life and death) is superior to any other person or religious system. His death is the perfect sacrifice with perfect results. In the old covenant, the blood of sacrificed animals was used again and again to purify all the things used in the tabernacle for worship (Hebrews 9:23; see Leviticus 16:14–20). All the priests had to be sprinkled with blood too (Exodus 29:20–21). Both objects and people were merely "copies of the heavenly things" (Hebrews 9:23), symbolising a more substantial reality in the heavenly realms. The heavenly things (not made with human hands—spiritual realities including the heavenly tabernacle and redeemed souls) are purified with "better sacrifices" (v. 23). This refers to Christ and His offering of himself as a sacrifice to do away with sin (v. 26).

Jesus did not offer ritual animal sacrifices for purification or bring their blood into the Holy of Holies (Hebrews 9:25). He never entered the Holy Place and the Holy of Holies in the temple on earth. Instead, we are reminded that the ministry of Christ takes place in the heavenly tabernacle (v. 24). He enters heaven on our behalf to "appear for us in God's presence" (v. 24), something that no Levitical priest or high priest was able to do. When Jesus died for us on the cross, the curtain in the temple (Exodus 26:33; Hebrews 9:3) that prevented anyone from entering the Holy of Holies (except the high priest once a year) was torn into two (Matthew 27:51). This was evidence that the death of Christ opened the way into God's presence for anyone who would believe in Jesus. His blood gives us all access to God (Hebrews 9:8; 10:19–20). Acts 6:7 records that "a large number of priests became obedient to the faith". Some of them may have even been eyewitnesses of the supernatural tearing of the curtain. **They realised that Jesus is the ultimate and real sacrifice that put an end to all the temple rituals.**

The death of Christ was "once for all"—there was no need for repeated sacrifices (Hebrews 9:25–26). All people must die once and then face judgment (v. 27). Likewise, Jesus died once but has risen and will "appear a second time, not to bear sin, but to bring salvation to those who are waiting for him" (v. 28)—to consummate the saving work begun by His death and resurrection. He saved us on the cross, is saving us now from the power of sin, and will ultimately save us from the presence of sin.

How does the writer spell out the unique features of Christ's offering of himself in the heavenly tabernacle? Why is Jesus the perfect sacrifice? Speak to Jesus with gratitude.

How are you waiting for His second coming? What salvation would He bring? What are the implications for your present walk with Christ?

Day 34

Read Hebrews 10:1–4

Imagine receiving a prescription from a doctor. He writes down the name of the medicine on the paper and then tells you, "This medicine will cure you." Now, you and I know that the piece of paper or the name of the medicine on it cannot do the actual healing. You would need to find a pharmacy or drug store to purchase the actual medicine, take it, and be healed. **For Jewish Christians to hang on to the rituals and sacrifices of the old covenant would be akin to the patient hanging on to the prescription paper for healing.** It is akin to not realising the difference between the prescription and the actual medicine.

It is a similar argument that the writer makes to help his readers to differentiate between the shadow and the substance, between the symbolic and real faith that produces spiritual transformation (Hebrews 10:1). The sacrifices in the tabernacle or temple had to be repeated endlessly because they were unable to "make perfect those who draw near to worship" (v. 1). It is similar to the patient who keeps looking at the prescription only to find that he is still not cured. In the same way, the annual sacrifices were an "annual reminder of sins" (v. 3) that refused to go away because one is not cleansed internally by the blood of sacrificial animals. They may purify one ritually, but not internally (v. 4). Coming back to our patient, suppose that even after getting the actual medicine from the pharmacy, he just looks daily at the prescription without ever taking the medicine! We would find that very odd.

In the same way, it was very odd that Jewish Christians, who now had Christ in their hearts, would be tempted to return to the ritual practices of Judaism. These practices were just shadows of the real Saviour and His perfect sacrifice for our sins. His sacrifice would take away the penalty, power, and one day, the very presence of sin once and for all. Why return to the prescription paper when the real medicine is now available?

ThinkThrough

Why was returning to old covenant practices not helpful when the Jewish Christians now worshipped Christ and followed Him? Is there any way we may do something similar in our lives? Think of the difference between relying on rituals and growing in a real relationship with Jesus.

What does the phrase "once for all" (Hebrews 10:2) mean for you? How do Christians show that they may not really believe in this, trying to supplement the finished work of Jesus on the cross? What can we do to avoid this?

Day 35

Read Hebrews 10:5–10

God had said through the Old Testament prophets, "I have no pleasure in the blood of bulls and lambs and goats" (Isaiah 1:11). Though He had instituted the temple sacrifices through Moses, He did not derive satisfaction and pleasure from them if they lacked the right attitude of obedience and worship (Hebrews 10:8). They were only a temporary measure to remind the Jews of the seriousness of sin and how life was to be poured out for the forgiveness of sin. However, animal blood was far from adequate for the task. **The river of animal blood that flowed in Jewish history pointed to the blood of Jesus that was shed outside Jerusalem and its temple.**

The blood of Jesus was effective because of His nature. He is no less than God, though He was also born into this world as a man. The blood of the God-Man has eternal value and power to bring forgiveness to humankind. Christ's sacrifice was unique both because of His identity and the way He carried it out.

The way Jews were to keep the law was through obedience. But they (like us) all failed, hence the need for the temple sacrificial rituals. Jesus was found without sin because He totally obeyed His Father in heaven.

The writer quotes the Septuagint version of Psalm 40:6–8 which can be directly applied to Christ (Hebrews 10:5–7). It reiterates that God is not fully satisfied with the sacrifice and offerings at the temple (v. 8). Instead He prepared a body for the Son of God. The significance of the quotation is then explained by the writer in verses 8 to 10.

The sacrifice of Jesus Christ (Hebrews 10:10) is effective and satisfied divine requirements because it came with voluntary self-giving love that was evidenced by total obedience. The commitment "I have come to do your will, my God" is applied uniquely to Jesus Christ (vv. 7, 9). In His ministry, Jesus constantly alluded to this (John 5:30; 6:38; 8:29). In the Garden of Gethsemane, Jesus said to the Father, "not as I will, but as you will" (Matthew 26:39). His willingness to be "obedient to death" on the cross was the subject matter of praise and worship in the early church (Philippians 2:8). It is through the once for all sacrifice of the body of Jesus that we "have been made holy" (Hebrews 10:10, the verb conveys an action with continuing results; see v. 14). No other sacrifice has such powerful and conclusive results.

Reflect on Isaiah 1:11, 1 Samuel 15:22, and Hebrews 9:13–14. In what way is the death of Christ both perfect obedience and sacrifice? Therefore, how is it contrasted with the temple sacrifices, and why does it make the temple sacrifices obsolete (Hebrews 10:9)?

What do you think the phrase "we have been made holy" (Hebrews 10:10) means? How does Jesus' sacrifice apply when we sin again and again (1 John 1:9)? How are you growing in the holiness that Christ has given you?

Day 36

Read Hebrews 10:11–18

The sacrifices related to Old Testament temple practices are contrasted with the one sufficient, self-giving sacrifice of Christ. The writer of Hebrews has already shown us the surpassing supremacy of Christ compared to the law, its tabernacle or temple, priesthood, sacrifices and rituals. On each count, Christ is incomparable. The Levitical priests stood "day after day" performing the same religious duties and offering "the same sacrifices", because they were only symbolic and "can never take away sins" (Hebrews 10:11). The phrase "this priest" refers to Jesus our High Priest, who had "offered for all time one sacrifice for sins" (v. 12). There was no further sacrifice needed because His sacrifice of himself was perfect and effective for ever. Having completed His perfect work of redeeming us, He therefore, "sat down at the right hand of God" (v. 12). His sitting (after completing His work) and the standing of the Levitical priest (who cannot do so) are clearly contrasted.[40]

Jesus meanwhile waits for the right time to return to establish His eternal kingdom, when His enemies will be made His footstool (Hebrews 10:13; see Psalm 110:1). He will have ultimate victory over all forces that are directed against God and His redemptive work. This is because Christ has already achieved sure victory through His sacrifice; "by one sacrifice he has made perfect for ever those who are being made holy" (Hebrews 10:14). This does not mean that we who are being made holy (a present ongoing process) are already perfect, as we all know from experience. **Rather, our future perfection is assured and guaranteed by what Christ has accomplished on the cross. This is good for eternity.**

The sacrifice of Jesus on the cross is God's definite means of forgiving our sins—for He will not remember our "sins and lawless acts" anymore when we are covered with the blood (1 Peter 1:1–2) and righteousness of Christ (Hebrews 10:17; see Jeremiah 31:34; Isaiah 61:10; Philippians 3:9). All this is part of the new covenant of Christ, through which God will bring His law into our hearts and minds (Hebrews 10:16; see Jeremiah 31:33). It will not only be on our lips (through reading the Bible), but deep in our hearts and minds (through meditation and understanding), so that we will be changed for ever (through obedience). In Christ, we would receive full and complete forgiveness and holiness—what could not be achieved by the old covenant.

[40] Hughes, *A Commentary on the Epistle to the Hebrews*, 400.

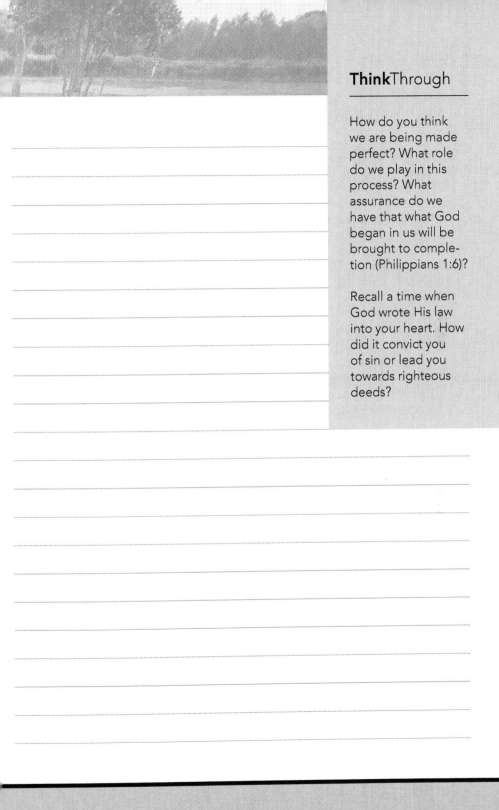

ThinkThrough

How do you think we are being made perfect? What role do we play in this process? What assurance do we have that what God began in us will be brought to completion (Philippians 1:6)?

Recall a time when God wrote His law into your heart. How did it convict you of sin or lead you towards righteous deeds?

Day 37

Read Hebrews 10:19–25

This passage begins with "therefore", referring to the previous discussion about the unique Melchizedek priesthood of Christ. It encourages readers to persevere in their faith in Christ. The previous truths are summarised in two "we have" statements. First, we have unshakeable "confidence to enter the Most Holy Place by the blood of Jesus" (Hebrews 10:19). Christ has opened up a new access into God's presence through the sacrifice of himself (His tortured body reflecting the tearing of the temple curtain; v. 20).[41] All this should help us respond with confident faith. Second, "we have a great priest" (v. 21) whose sacrifice has brought inner cleansing (of the conscience; v. 22). The phrase "having our bodies washed with pure water" (v. 22) refers to baptism, a sign of the inner spiritual cleansing from sin (see Ephesians 5:26 and Titus 3:5).

After reiterating these central truths, the passage goes on to three exhortations beginning with the phrase "Let us". First, we must "draw near to God" (Hebrews 10:22). Second, we are to hold "unswervingly to the hope we profess" (v. 23). The word for "profess" is *homologia*, which means "rang out" (see 1 Thessalonians 1:8). **Our proclamation of the gospel of Jesus must grow in conviction, because God is faithful.** Third, "let us consider how we may spur one another on towards love and good deeds" (v. 24). Confident of God's work for us in Christ, we can then as God's "fellow workers" (1 Corinthians 3:9), do all good works that God has prepared for us in Christ (Ephesians 2:10). Such works must be motivated by God's love. As Christians, we are responsible to encourage one another to live in this way. Continuing on to verse 25, we must "not [give] up meeting together". This is necessary for us to remain in Christ. This is a vital source of strength to help us remain faithful to Christ. Some of the original readers were apparently neglecting the spiritual discipline of gathering in the church for worship, prayer, teaching, and mutual encouragement.

There is no such thing as lone ranger Christianity, for we are all baptised into the body of Christ (1 Corinthians 12:13). There is danger in neglecting community life,[42] for our faith can become shaky as we forget the great truths about Christ that are meant to be repeated in church meetings. We must meet together so that we can encourage one another toward love and good deeds, especially since the return of Christ is approaching (Hebrews 10:25). There should be a sense of expectation and urgency.

[41] Hughes, *A Commentary on the Epistle to the Hebrews*, 410.

[42] D. Stephen Long, *Hebrews* (Louisville, KY: Westminster John Knox Press, 2011), 243–244.

ThinkThrough

Consider the two "we have" statements (Hebrews 10:19, 21). They speak of our competent High Priest and the resulting confident faith we should have. Reflect on these truths and pray them into your life.

Reflect on the three "we have" exhortations in relation to your discipleship. Which of these are most needed for you? How important is corporate worship and fellowship, and how can you encourage faltering fellow Christians?

Day 38

Read Hebrews 10:26–31

This passage is the fourth warning in the book (the first three are in Hebrews 2:1–3; 3:12–19; 6:4–6)—it warns against falling into apostasy. If people (the author includes himself with the "we") who profess to be Christians "deliberately keep on sinning" they have spurned God (Hebrews 10:26). They should know better, "[having] received the knowledge of the truth". **But knowledge must result in obedience; otherwise it will only serve to condemn us on the day of judgment.** For such people, "no sacrifice for sins is left", meaning that since they have rejected the sacrifice of Christ, there is no other way for them to receive salvation (Acts 4:12; 1 John 5:11–12). What awaits them is a terrifying judgment of fire that is kept for the enemies of God (Hebrews 10:27; Isaiah 26:11).

Those who wilfully broke the law of Moses were judged ("died without mercy") on the evidence of two or three witnesses (Hebrews 10:28; see Deuteronomy 17:6). But those who reject Christ are guilty of more serious offences, and therefore will be more severely punished. First, they would have "trampled the Son of God underfoot" (Hebrews 10:29)—a terrible rebellion against the one who is Lord and King. Such people will belong to the enemies of God who will become the footstool of Christ (v. 13). Second, they would have "treated as an unholy thing the blood of the covenant" that sanctifies us (v. 29). This is to make the blood of Jesus as common as any other kind of blood, and to belittle the great sacrifice He made of himself. Third, they would have "insulted the Spirit of grace" (v. 29). Jesus warned about the unpardonable sin against the Holy Spirit which would not be forgiven "either in this age or in the age to come" (Matthew 12:30–32). To reject the good news about Christ is to insult the Holy Spirit who brings that message.

We must not take God for granted. He is merciful and kind to us and has treated us with love and grace. But we must remember that God is both kind and stern (Romans 11:22). Christ is not only the sacrifice for our sins but also our coming Judge. To reject Him as Saviour is to face His severe judgment in the future. "To deny Christ is to choose judgment."[43] It is indeed "a dreadful thing to fall into the hands of the living God" (Hebrews 10:31) when we are without Christ.

[43] Healy, *Hebrews*, 217.

What is the difference between "deliberately keep on sinning" (Hebrews 10:26) and to fall into sin occasionally? Why is it that a deliberate sinner who continues to sin neither knows Jesus, nor is in Him (1 John 3:6)?

Consider how you would stand before Christ in judgment? What should reassure you? How can you guard against taking your salvation for granted?

Day 39

Read Hebrews 10:32–39

Having called for confidence in the truths about Jesus as our High Priest and Saviour and cautioned against leaving these truths, the author now urges his original readers to persevere in their faith in Christ (Hebrews 10:36). Most of the Jewish Christians were thankfully faithful to Christ, though there were some who had already drifted away from their faith into apostasy. They had left the Christian faith to return to Judaism because they would thus escape the severe persecution directed at Christians.

Thus far, the writer has written persuasively about the unshakeable truths about Christ and the foolishness of drifting away from Him. Lest those who had remained faithful thus far be tempted to drift away as well, the writer reminds them of how they "received the light" (responded to the gospel) and stood firmly in their faith amid great persecution and suffering (Hebrews 10:32). They had been persecuted in several ways (vv. 33–34). They were publicly insulted. Some were imprisoned; some had their properties confiscated. In all of this they had stood firm and in solidarity with their suffering brethren. They knew that even if they lost their earthly possessions, they would inherit lasting possessions if they were faithful (v. 34; see 1 Peter 1:4).

The writer urges the remaining steadfast believers not to throw away their confidence in Christ (Hebrews 10:35), and assures them that their faithfulness will be rewarded. **They need to persevere in their faith and obedience to the will of God (v. 36). God will reward such steady faith.** The author combines the Septuagint version of Habakkuk 2:3 with Isaiah 26:21, substituting "the revelation" with "he who is coming" (Hebrews 10:37). Christ is coming "in just a little while" (v. 37)—which to any believer in the midst of persecution and suffering would provide much faith and encouragement.

This book addresses two types of people who profess to be Christians: those who "[shrink] back" and those who persevere in faith (Hebrews 10:38–39). The first group are headed for serious trouble (God will not be pleased with them; they will be destroyed). The second group will be saved. Jesus did teach about the broad and narrow way. The broad way may appear easy and more comfortable to travel on but it "leads to destruction" (Matthew 7:13). The narrow road is a more difficult path to travel, and few travel on it but it "leads to life" (Matthew 7:14). We have to make the right choice.

Reflect on the persecution that the original readers of Hebrews had experienced. How are they encouraged by the writer? What forms of loss and suffering have you experienced? Read John 16:33. How does Christ's promise help you?

How might Christians shrink back when it becomes difficult to remain faithful to Christ? What can they do when tempted in this way?

Day 40

Read Hebrews 11:1–3

Chapter 10 closes with the declaration that the righteous live by faith, thus setting the stage for a great discussion on faith.

Faith is defined here as "confidence in what we hope for and assurance about what we do not see" (Hebrews 11:1). First, faith has to do with that which is invisible. Paul tells us that what is seen is only temporary, unlike that which is unseen, which is eternal (2 Corinthians 4:18). Many people live pragmatically; they live and make decisions on the basis of what they can see. They are like the rich fool who planned for his business expansion and wealth management without paying attention to spiritual realities. He did not know he would die soon (Luke 12:16–21). Such people live by sight, not by faith (see 2 Corinthians 5:7), because they are either ignorant of the invisible spiritual realities or ignore them. God is the greatest reality in the universe, and to ignore Him is to condemn ourselves to a meaningless life. Only when we recognise that God is in the centre of what we cannot see, do we really learn to live. This faith comes from hearing (Romans 10:17), for though we cannot see the invisible God, we can hear Him (usually through His Word). **We live by faith when we choose to live by what we hear from God rather than what we see in the world.**

Faith is also defined as "confidence in what we hope for" (Hebrews 11:1). This world offers all kinds of hope. People hope for a better job, a better house, better health, and the like. Some get what they hope for. But the kind of hope this passage speaks about does not belong to this world. It has to do with what lies in the future when Christ will return: a new earth and heaven. This will become clearer in the following passages. Paul writes that it is "in this hope we were saved" (Romans 8:24). He continues, "But hope that is seen is no hope at all. Who hopes for what they already have? But if we hope for what we do not yet have, we wait for it patiently" (Romans 8:24–25).

Such faith recognises the unseen God as the creator of all that is seen (Hebrews 11:3). He created everything *ex nihilo* (out of nothing) and is at the heart of all reality. "For in him we live and move and have our being" (Acts 17:28).

ThinkThrough

How does worldly pragmatism affect faith? How can faith in the invisible God be expressed in our daily lives? How would you assess your faith in this regard?

What are your real hopes in life? How much of them are related with things that go beyond this world? What difference would it make?

Day 41

Read Hebrews 11:4–7

Following the definition of faith, we are presented with a host of Old Testament people who demonstrated faith in their lives. This passage focuses on a few persons who preceded Abraham, the father of faith: Abel, Enoch, and Noah.

Abel was Adam's son who was murdered by his jealous brother Cain. Abel kept flocks and Cain planted crops (Genesis 4:2). Both brought offerings for the Lord. The Lord "looked with favour on Abel and his offering, but on Cain and his offering he did not look with favour" (Genesis 4:4–5). God looked at not just the offerings but also the men who brought them. Abel was acceptable but Cain, for some reason (perhaps his heart and attitude were wrong), was not. Tragically, Cain then murdered his brother in cold blood (Genesis 4:8). Abel is commended here because he was a "righteous" man who brought "a better offering" (v. 4). **His life was marked by faith, and he continues to appeal to others to have faith.**

It was by faith that Enoch "walked faithfully with God" (Genesis 5:22, 24). He did not die the usual way, but after living for 365 years, he "was no more, because God took him away" (Genesis 5:24) straight to heaven—like the prophet Elijah (2 Kings 2:1, 11). A change came about in Enoch after the birth of his son Methuselah (which means "His death shall bring it"). It appears that God revealed to Enoch the coming flood that would put an end to the widespread wickedness in the world. It changed the man because after Methuselah's birth, he walked with God (suggesting a turning to God by faith and a growing intimacy maintained by faith; Genesis 5:22). According to the chronology in Genesis 5, the flood indeed came when Methuselah died.[44] The author notes that Enoch had pleased God before being taken away, and since "without faith it is impossible to please God" (Hebrews 11:6), he emphasises that Enoch demonstrated faith.

Noah's story is also one of faith amid social ridicule and wickedness (Genesis 6:9–9:17). Like Enoch, Noah too "walked faithfully with God" (Genesis 6:9); he was a righteous man who "did everything just as God commanded him" (Genesis 6:22; 7:5). He built the ark as an act of faith (taking God's warning of a great flood seriously) and saved his family and the animals. He saw things not yet seen, and feared God (Hebrews 11:7). He was saved through his faith in God and thus "became heir of the righteousness that is in keeping with faith" (v. 7).

[44] Stedman, *Hebrews*, 120.

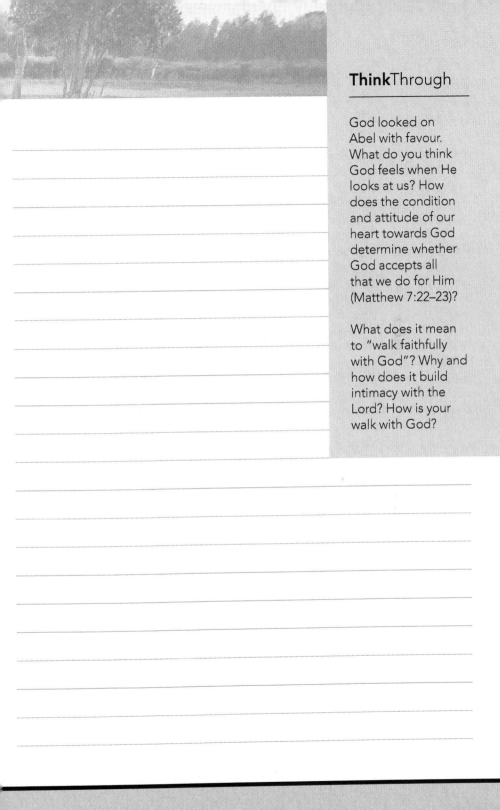

God looked on Abel with favour. What do you think God feels when He looks at us? How does the condition and attitude of our heart towards God determine whether God accepts all that we do for Him (Matthew 7:22–23)?

What does it mean to "walk faithfully with God"? Why and how does it build intimacy with the Lord? How is your walk with God?

Day 42

Read Hebrews 11:8–19

The story of Abraham is a story of faith, though at times Abraham faltered (see Genesis 20). Three things are highlighted in Abraham's long story. They are introduced with the phrase "By faith". First, Abraham left the comfort and security of his home in pagan Ur for a place God would show him (Hebrews 11:8–9). He had not seen God's Promised Land before (no glossy brochures then!); he simply believed God, packed up his things, and went. Second, it was *by faith* that Abraham believed God's impossible-sounding promise that in their old age, he and Sarah would have a son (v. 11). And from Isaac would come many more descendants. Third, it was *by faith* that Abraham was willing to obey God by offering his precious one and only son Isaac as a sacrifice (v. 17). How was God going to keep His promise about blessing Abraham with countless descendants if the only way that could happen— through Isaac—was going to be taken away from him? But Abraham trusted God and believed that God was able to raise the dead (v. 19).

It is in these three ways that Abraham stands out as a man of faith—in leaving comfort for the unknown, in believing God for the impossible, and in obeying God by his willingness to give up the very means of his blessings.

In this sense, Abraham is the "father of us all" (Romans 4:16), all who have faith. All these people, including Abraham and Sarah, were still living by faith when they died (Hebrews 11:13). It is not that they obtained all of God's promises on earth. They knew they were just passing through to "a better country—a heavenly one" that had been prepared for them by God himself (v. 16).

Thus, Abraham lived in tents (Hebrews 11:9, showing he was a pilgrim on earth). He believed that his ultimate destination was not on earth. Even when he arrived in Canaan, the Promised Land flowing with milk and honey (Exodus 3:8), he experienced famine (Genesis 12:10). His descendants also suffered famine (Genesis 26:1; 43:1). Did God short-change them? No, this was an indication to Abraham and the others that God's promises had to do with more than just the land. It was spiritual reality more than just geography and agriculture. One needs faith to believe this and live accordingly with "single-minded commitment".[45]

[45] Hughes, *A Commentary on the Epistle to the Hebrews*, 481.

ThinkThrough

Consider these three events connected with Abraham that are highlighted here as evidence of faith. Which of these is most inspiring to you? When is it difficult to apply faith?

Why is it important to look beyond the things of this world? What are your own thoughts on the "better country" (Hebrews 11:16), the city "whose architect and builder is God" (v. 10)? How do you nurture your longing for this heavenly country?

Day 43

Read Hebrews 11:20–22

Abraham's son (Isaac), grandson (Jacob), and great grandson (Joseph) are highlighted in this passage as men who had faith. It is by faith that Isaac blessed Jacob and Esau "in regard to their future" (Hebrews 11:20). The actual event is a sad tale of deception within the family and the unholy ambition of Rebecca (Isaac's wife) and Jacob the deceiving son. Jacob tricked blind Isaac into giving him the blessing meant for his brother, Esau (Genesis 27). Nearing death, Isaac acted in faith as he blessed both his sons for the future. Though he was deceived by Jacob, by divine providence he was able to predict accurately what would happen to his two sons.

Likewise, Jacob, "when he was dying, blessed each of Joseph's sons, and worshipped as he leaned on the top of his staff" (Hebrews 11:21; see Genesis 47:31). Joseph had been sold as a slave by his jealous brothers, but God raised him up to be next in rank to the Pharaoh in Egypt. When the rest of the family was brought to Egypt to escape the famine, Jacob knew that he would die soon and blessed Joseph's two sons, Manasseh (the older) and Ephraim (Genesis 48:8–20). Jacob could hardly see because of old age, and Joseph placed his two sons so that Manasseh could be blessed with Jacob's right hand and Ephraim

with his left hand. The idea was that the right hand had better blessings. But Jacob crossed his hands and gave the younger boy Ephraim his greater blessing. Joseph was "displeased" (Genesis 48:17) but Jacob maintained his blessings. By faith, Jacob understood God's choice of blessing the younger over the older. So like his father Isaac, he blessed the younger Ephraim over the older Manasseh. He also favoured Joseph over firstborn Reuben when blessing each of his own sons (Genesis 49). All this was done by a faith that could see the future.

Joseph, too, acted in faith as he approached death in his old age (Hebrews 11:22). He could see by faith that Egypt was not the permanent home of Israel's sons. He told his brothers, "I am about to die" and that "God will surely come to your aid and take you up out of this land to the land he promised on oath to Abraham, Isaac and Jacob" (Genesis 50:24). By faith he saw the Exodus event led by God and gave instructions for his bones to be brought to the Promised Land (Hebrews 11:22; Genesis 50:24–25). This was fulfilled (Joshua 24:32). **Through faith, all three patriarchs trusted in God's promises for the future.**

ThinkThrough

Why is faith necessary in helping us face death? How will faith enable us to trust God for the future? How does one nurture such faith?

If Abraham saw what lay ahead in heaven, the other patriarchs saw what lay ahead on earth. Both visions require faith. How do you exercise such faith?

Day 44

Read Hebrews 11:23–28

The focus of this passage is Moses, the greatest figure next to Abraham in Jewish history. His parents responded with faith when the new anti-Israelite Pharaoh ordered all newborn boys to be thrown into the Nile to be killed. Like the Hebrew midwives who disobeyed the king's command to kill baby boys because they feared the Lord (Exodus 1:17), Moses' parents feared God and not the king (Hebrews 11:23). They hid their son because they saw "he was no ordinary child" (v. 23). The ancient Jewish writer Josephus, who recorded the history of the Jews, suggested that the parents were told by God about their son's destiny.[46] They feared and believed God.

Moses shared his parents' faith. Though he was brought up as the son of the Egyptian princess, and could have inherited much including the throne (Exodus 2:1–10), he threw away his royal identity (Hebrews 11:24) to be a leader of the Jews. He intervened and killed an Egyptian slave master who was ruthlessly beating a Hebrew slave and had to flee for safety (Exodus 2:11–15). He chose to stand by his Hebrew people, and preferred mistreatment rather than sinful pleasures, disgrace for the sake of Christ (though Christ was to come much later in history) rather than Egypt's treasures

(Hebrews 11:25–26). **By faith, his eyes were on distant rewards rather than present fame and comfort (v. 26).** Therefore, by faith, he left Egypt.

By faith, Moses "saw him who is invisible" (v. 27). How does one see the invisible one? This could refer to Moses' burning bush experience (Exodus 3:1–6). He could have passed the bush countless times, but one day his eyes were opened to see God and hear Him. It could also refer to later on, when Moses expressed an intense desire to see God's glory (Exodus 33:18). The man had great faith in responding to whatever God told him and showed him. His leadership of the Hebrews in very difficult circumstances, his courage in challenging the pharaoh, and the plagues he brought to Egypt in judgment of Egypt's many gods (Exodus 12:12) show his great faith in God. Moses again showed his faith by instructing the people to sacrifice the Passover lamb, just as God had commanded him (Hebrews 11:28; see Exodus 12:21).

[46] Stedman, *Hebrews*, 128.

ThinkThrough

Why is faith needed to leave the glitter and passing glories of this earth for something you cannot see yet? Do you need to exercise faith in your current situation to let go of the transient so as to take hold of the eternal?

What does it mean to see the invisible? How do you experience this in daily life? What would be the result?

Day 45

Read Hebrews 11:29–31

The Bible records many times when God performed miracles in response to faith. One of the greatest tests that the Israelites faced when they left Egypt was being trapped between the sea and the advancing Egyptian army that was pursuing them after the pharaoh changed his mind (Hebrews 11:29). It was a "between the devil and the deep blue sea" kind of situation. The Israelites were terrified and cried out to God (Exodus 14:10). They scolded Moses for bringing them to a dead end and expressed willingness to return to their slavery in Egypt (Exodus 14:12)! **But Moses responded with unshakeable faith, encouraging the people to stand firm, for God would fight for them.** He obeyed God by lifting his staff over the sea, and God miraculously parted the Red Sea to make a way for the Israelites to proceed. The Egyptian army perished in the sea when they tried to follow the Israelites. When the people saw this, they "feared the Lord and put their trust in him and in Moses his servant" (Exodus 14:31).

The scene shifts forward to Joshua leading the Israelites into Canaan (Hebrews 11:30). Their first big hurdle was the well-fortified city of Jericho. They had no means to overcome the ancient city, but God gave them instructions that showed how they could conquer the city His way. They were told to march around the city for seven days (Joshua 5:13–6:27). They could have been the laughing stock of the people of Jericho, but they had faith to obey God when He promised to deliver the city into their hands. Their unusual act of faith brought the thick city walls down.

Then there is the story of Rahab, a prostitute in Jericho (Hebrews 11:31). Joshua had sent two spies into the city. When they were pursued, she hid and protected them. She expressed faith in God by saying, "the Lord your God is God in heaven above and on the earth below" and "'I know that the Lord has given this land to you" (Joshua 2:11, 9). She asked to be spared when Jericho is conquered. For her faith, she was saved by the Israelites. Actually, it was God who saved her and her family, for the part of the wall where her house stood did not collapse (Joshua 2:15; 6:22).

Reflect on the difference between the faith of the Exodus generation and that of Moses. When caught in a corner, what is your usual response? When was the last time you experienced one of God's miracles in what seemed an impossible situation? How did your faith play a part in it?

Rahab, a non-Israelite, was saved and honoured for her faith. She became the great grandmother of King David (Matthew 1:5–6). What does this say about the effects of faith?

Day 46

Read Hebrews 11:32–38

Not to overwhelm the reader with more wonderful examples of faith from the Old Testament, the writer brings his list to a summarised conclusion. He mentions six more names (Gideon, Barak, Samson, Jephthah, David, and Samuel), without going into detail, ranging from the judges to the early monarchs. Prophets are also included. Their achievements, carried out by faith, are summarised (Hebrews 11:33–35). They "conquered kingdoms" (Judges 7–8; 11:29; 2 Samuel 8:1–3), "administered justice" (1 Samuel 7:15–17) and "gained what was promised" (Joshua 21:43). They "shut the mouths of lions" (Daniel 6:22), "quenched the fury of the flames" (Daniel 3:17) and "escaped the edge of the sword" (2 Kings 6:11–18). Their "weakness was turned to strength" (Judges 16:30; 1 Samuel 14:14). They were powerful in battle and "routed foreign armies" (Judges 4–5). "Women received back their dead" (1 Kings 17:22–23; 2 Kings 4:8–37). All these were achieved by faith.

But faith does not always bring success and victory; it also gives strong endurance amid persecution and suffering. The writer includes in his list "others who were tortured, refusing to be released"—they preferred to die and be resurrected than deny their faith in God (Hebrews 11:35). The list of sufferings of the martyrs is tragic and inspiring at the same time (vv. 36–38): some faced "jeers and flogging" (Jeremiah 20:2; 37:15); others were "chained" and imprisoned, "stoned" (2 Chronicles 24:21), "sawed in two" and "put to death by the sword" (1 Kings 19:10). They were reduced to poverty and were persecuted, seeking safety in deserts, mountains, caves, and holes in the ground. The writer summarised their exemplary faith and righteousness by saying "the world was not worthy of them" (Hebrews 11:38).

By the time the author comes to this point, his readers no doubt were stirred in their faith as they surveyed the gallery of heroes of the faith. **Such a tour is necessary today, for we have many more examples from the history of the church: martyrs, monks, missionaries, and ordinary Christians whose lives exhibited the reality and the power of God as they placed their faith in Him, in trust and obedience.** Reading good Christian biography will help us to do this.

Think of some examples of faith in Christian history that you may know about. What lessons can you learn from them?

In what way is your faith helping you to do great things for God, and in what way is it helping you to endure hardship? If you are included in the gallery of faith, what will you be remembered for?

Day 47

Read Hebrews 11:39–40

All those mentioned in Hebrews 11, whether named or unnamed, "were all commended for their faith" (Hebrews 11:39; see vv. 2, 4). Firstly, they were commended by God himself. It was God who commended Abel as a righteous man (v. 4). **God was pleased to be called the God of the faithful, who had set their eyes ultimately on invisible realities and destinations (v. 16).** Second, these were commended by the people of faith. They were recognised for their faith and faithfulness to God, so much so that the writer creates a "Hall of Faith" in chapter 11. The writer himself gives the verdict that those who suffered for their faith were outstanding, as "the world was not worthy of them" (v. 38).

Yet "none of them received what had been promised" (Hebrews 11:39). This does not mean that they were not blessed or failed to experience God's presence and power. What this refers to is the fullness of God's promises in Christ. While they had faith in God's promises, they had to wait for the appearance of Christ to receive the fullness of God's blessings (Ephesians 1:3). They "did not receive the things promised; they only saw them and welcomed them from a distance" (Hebrews 11:13). The writer assures his original Jewish Christian readers that "God had planned something better for us" (v. 40). They had the advantage of knowing Christ which their forefathers did not have. Hebrews establishes the superiority of Christ above all the old religious systems of the Jews, valid as they were for a period. But now that Christ has come, He has replaced all the shadows of the past with His reality. The faith of the fathers was not wasted, though. There was continuity between their faith in a distant Messiah and the faith of the Christians who had heard and experienced this Messiah. This was the "something better" that the text indicates. French theologian John Calvin challenges us that while "a tiny spark of light led them to heaven", we who have "the Sun of righteousness" shining on us have no excuse to "still cling to the earth".[47]

The splendid truth is that "only together with us would [the heroes of faith] be made perfect" (Hebrews 11:40), by experiencing purification from sin at the resurrection. God has a single plan for all of us—in Christ.[48]

[47] Stedman, *Hebrews*, 135.
[48] Hughes, *A Commentary on the Epistle to the Hebrews*, 516.

How do you think
God would com-
mend your faith? If
you lack faith, ask
Him to help you
(see Mark 9:24).

Reflect on Calvin's
point. In what ways
do Christians cling
to the earth? How
should our choices
be even better than
those of the Old
Testament saints?

Day 48

Read Hebrews 12:1–2

Chapter 12 begins with "therefore", showing that a visit to the Hall of Faith should inspire us to run the race of Christian faith with renewed commitment and perseverance. It is not a race that we decide for ourselves, but is "marked out for us" (Hebrews 12:1). This means that we have to run the race "according to the rules" (2 Timothy 2:5). One such rule is that we must exercise faith by trusting and obeying God even if the circumstances are against us. Another is that we cannot run the race faithfully unless we nurture a growing relationship with Christ through spiritual disciplines such as regular Bible reading and prayer, worship and service. We must also accept that suffering is very much a part of this race; we must not be detracted by suffering but allow God to build in us perseverance, character, and hope through it (Romans 5:3–4). All these are examples of what it means to run the race God has assigned to us according to the rules.

We do not run in a vacuum or alone. We are "surrounded by such a great cloud of witnesses" (Hebrews 12:1). For the original readers of Hebrews, this would be the Old Testament heroes of faith. For us, this would include all believers whose example inspires us onward. Imagine a relay race.[49] We are like the present runner, who is cheered by his teammates who have finished their part and are waiting for their team to win. The baton is in our hand, and we must run well as we are cheered on. Only when the last runner has run and won the race will the whole team receive the medal (see Hebrews 11:40). While the verse probably does not mean that those who have gone before us are watching us from above, the idea inspires us to run well. **Above all, God is watching us, and enabling us to run well. We are to "fix our eyes on Jesus" (12:2; a central theme in Hebrews) as we run.** Jesus is the author (or pioneer, who ran before us, and now runs with us in every race) and perfecter of our faith. He is our model, motivator, and companion in the race. He sets the race, as we follow Him—enduring the cross, scorning its shame, and joining Him at the Father's right hand (see Ephesians 2:6).

We must therefore discard anything that hinders us by trapping us in sin (Hebrews 12:1) so that we can run well. Sin and even things acceptable on their own (such as hobbies) must go if they hold us back.

[49] Morris, "Hebrews", 133.

How do you keep your eyes on Jesus? What external distractions make you turn your eyes away from Him? What can you do to avoid these distractions?

What inner hindrances in your life prevent you from running well in your Christian disciple-ship? What may need to be discarded? Be honest and firm with yourself. Turn your thoughts into prayer.

Day 49

Read Hebrews 12:3–4

Keeping our eyes fixed on Jesus, we are urged to "consider him" (Hebrews 12:3). The Greek word *analogizomai* means "to think over, ponder, weigh, compare". Think about Him. Remember and recognise who He is. Keep looking at Him as your Saviour and High Priest, and as your perfect example. For the second time in chapter 12, the author highlights the endurance of Jesus. He endured the cross (v. 2) and "such opposition from sinners" (v. 3). The Greek word for endure is *hypomenō*, which literally means "to remain or abide under" and "to patiently suffer". Jesus is the perfect example of such strong endurance; no amount of opposition and suffering would detract Him from the cross. He was unmoved, remaining in a position of obedience no matter how fierce the battle. We are to look to Him, especially when the going gets very tough, and we are tempted to give up or give in. Peter reminds us that "Christ suffered for you, leaving you an example, that you should follow in his steps" (1 Peter 2:21). When He was insulted and tortured, He "entrusted himself to him who judges justly" (1 Peter 2:23). This is how Jesus endured, and this is how we, too, should endure amid fierce opposition and intense suffering.

Two things must be avoided. We should not "grow weary" and we should not "lose heart" (Hebrews 12:3). With relentless suffering, one can get tired and give up, but in Christ we should not. Jesus commended the church in Ephesus, "You have persevered and have endured hardships for my name, and have not grown weary" (Revelation 2:3). To lose heart is to lose our courage and our resolve—which can happen when we turn our eyes away from Christ to focus on the overwhelming waves and buffeting winds (see Matthew 14:30). **Because Paul was able to keep his eyes on Jesus, he was able to declare "we do not lose heart" (2 Corinthians 4:1, 16).** We too can say the same if we look to Jesus, for God has promised that those who hope in the Lord will not grow weary and not be faint (Isaiah 40:31).

The writer brings the focus to the "struggle against sin" (Hebrews 12:4), indicating both our own sin and external trials and persecution, that often causes us pain and suffering and tempts us to give up. He tells his readers that they "have not yet resisted to the point of shedding your blood" (v. 4), as Jesus did. They must therefore take heart and follow Him faithfully.

ThinkThrough

How would you "consider" Jesus? Write down your thoughts and turn them into prayer.

Is there any area in your "struggle against sin" where you feel weariness and a loss of heart? What would your prayer be in this regard? What do you think the Lord would say to you?

Day 50

Read Hebrews 12:5–11

Keeping our thoughts on how hard Christian discipleship can be, the writer asks his possibly weary readers, "Have you completely forgotten this word of encouragement that addresses you as a father addresses his son?" (Hebrews 12:5). The writer quotes Proverbs 3:11–12 to give an unusual encouragement to those in the midst of suffering. It does not promise a bed of roses, but offers meaning and hope. It points to the "Lord's discipline" (Hebrews 12:5) which involves His verbal rebuke and a more painful punishment (literally scourging)—a lesson that is not easily forgotten. The recipient of such discipline can remember that this means he is God's true son, whom God is shaping for future service, unlike those who are not His children (vv. 7–8), who have rejected such discipline. Those who seem to have no struggles may not be the genuine children of God (see Psalm 73).

We all have earthly fathers who disciplined us when we were children, and though they are imperfect, we appreciate them for disciplining us and shaping our character. How much more will the "Father of [our] spirits", our heavenly Father who gives us spiritual life and who loves us perfectly, discipline us for our own good (Hebrews 12:9).

Our earthly fathers did what they thought was best "for a little while", but our heavenly Father would, in His wisdom and love, discipline us "that we may share in his holiness" (Hebrews 12:10). The way God disciplines us is intended to make us share His character, to "participate in the divine nature" (2 Peter 1:4). As it has been said, there is no gain without pain, no crown without a cross.

As we struggle with sin, and as we persevere through persecution and pain, we are gaining ground and making steady progress. Though it is hard to bear, we can take heart that it provides spiritual training ("trained by it", *gymnazō* in Greek, from which we get "gymnasium") for our souls and will produce a "harvest of righteousness and peace" (Hebrews 12:11; see Isaiah 32:17; James 3:17–18)—of right living and right relationships. These thoughts are most comforting when we are going through a painful trial. First, we remember that we are God's children and He loves us. Second, we know that "in all things God works for the good of those who love him, who have been called according to his purpose" (Romans 8:28). We can trust in God's love for us and in His wise and sovereign purposes.

ThinkThrough

Think of God's discipline (and training) in your life. How have you experienced it and what does it say about your relationship to God? Think of how God's firmness expresses His love for you.

What "harvest of righteousness and peace" have you already seen in your life? What more can you expect from the training God is putting you through? What sort of trainee are you?

Day 51

Read Hebrews 12:12–17

Several practical imperatives follow one another in rapid succession. First, we must strengthen our "feeble arms and weak knees" (Hebrews 12:12; Isaiah 35:3), not with our own strength but by looking to God's promises. **The word "strengthen" is in the plural, meaning that it is a collective action as we mutually encourage one another to lean upon the sturdy and steady presence of God.** As we take care of our own lives, we will also be a blessing to others. We are to "make level paths" (Hebrews 12:13; see Proverbs 4:26–27), choosing to live godly lives by staying obedient to God's Word, "so that the lame may not be disabled, but rather healed" (Hebrews 12:13)—those fellow believers who are weak and about to give up.

Then we must also ensure that we live both in peace (our social relationships) and holiness (our relationship with God; v. 14). Living in peace must be with "everyone" (at least we should try hard, see Romans 12:18; Hebrews 12:14). Holiness must be pursued because without it "no one will see the Lord" (Hebrews 12:14). We must guard against apostasy, for fear of missing the grace of God (v. 15; see Galatians 5:4). Another key danger is allowing "bitter root[s]" to grow in our lives (v. 15; see Deuteronomy 29:18).

Such bitter roots may be connected with idolatry, as the Deuteronomy passage shows. The problem is that when the heart turns away, we will stray from the life-giving presence of the Lord.

Another example of bitter roots is to remain in sexual immorality (Hebrews 12:16), which was often connected with idolatry (Exodus 32; Hosea 4:12–14; Revelation 2:14, 20). It could also be simply a love for material pleasures, even legitimate ones such as food (which can become gluttony), or possessions (which can become greed). The example of Esau is mentioned as one who gave in to his hungry desires and traded his inheritance rights for them (Hebrews 12:16; Genesis 25:29–35). He gave up an eternal blessing for a fleeting pleasure. It was too late for Esau when he pleaded for the blessing he had so carelessly thrown away (Genesis 27:38).

It is vital that we identify bitter roots growing within us that will "cause trouble and defile" (Hebrews 12:15). If we find any unconfessed sin, persistent sinful habits, unholy desires and ambitions, and unresolved grudges and rage within us, we should pull them out—roots and all (Colossians 3:5–8). We should make sure that we do not hide inner bitterness and bondage to sin, even in our religious acts (Acts 8:23).

ThinkThrough

How can we strengthen our feeble hands and weak knees? Why is doing this in community so helpful? Consider if you are a stumbling block to others in any way.

Reflect on bitter roots that exist within. See if you can find any within your heart. What would you do about them?

Day 52

Read Hebrews 12:18–24

In contrasting the old covenant and the new, the author uses two striking pictures. He refers to two mountains: Mount Sinai and Mount Zion. Mount Sinai represents the old covenant, where the law of Moses was given (Exodus 19). It was the fearful experience of God's holy presence that made the mountain out of bounds except to Moses and a few chosen leaders. The mountaintop itself was restricted to Moses. Any infraction would be met with instant death. Such was the terror of the mountain (Hebrews 12:20). Even Moses trembled with fear (v. 21). **Mount Sinai reminds us how far we are from God and how terribly fallen we are. That is the purpose of the law. There is no relief for us there.**

The other mountain (Zion) represents the heavenly Jerusalem (Hebrews 12:22). It brings us to God's grace and glory, healing and salvation. When we arrive at Mount Zion, we have arrived at the city which Abraham longed for (11:10), where countless angels are joyfully present (12:22). We would have arrived where the "church of the firstborn, whose names are written in heaven" is (v. 23), made up of privileged sons and daughters of God through the work of Jesus the firstborn Son (Hebrews 1:6; 2:10–17; Romans 8:29; Colossians 1:18; Revelation 1:5). We would have "come to God, the Judge of all" (Hebrews 12:23). We would have come to "the spirits of the righteous made perfect" (v. 23), both the pre-Christian people of faith (see Hebrews 11:40) and Christian era saints.[50] We would have come to Jesus, "the mediator of a new covenant" (12:24). We would have come to His "sprinkled blood that speaks a better word than the blood of Abel" (v. 24); an invitation to forgiveness, not a cry for justice. While the blood of Abel seeks justice, the blood of Jesus seeks atonement to bring God's forgiveness, peace, and salvation. In so many words, and such a poetic flow of words and images, the author shows the striking contrast between the old and new covenants. The new covenant is centred in the Person and work of Christ. It is He who brings us to God and His redeemed and perfected people, and to an eternity filled with God's glory and peace.

This is reason enough for any Jewish Christian who may be contemplating leaving their faith in Christ to not return to the old Jewish religion. Why run to the law to find grace when we should run to grace to find the law? We will not be saved by trusting in our obedience to God's law. But when we trust in Christ and receive His grace, we can then be saved and given God's help to obey His law.

[50] Bruce, *Epistle to the Hebrews*, 376–377.

What does Mount
Sinai remind you
of? What is the
difference between
fearing God and
being terrified of
Him? What sort of
religious experience
will each produce?

What does Mount
Zion remind you of?
Reflect on how the
writer describes it. Is
there a place still for
the law, or should we
discard it?

Day 53

Read Hebrews 12:25–29

This is the fifth and final warning in the book (the others are in Hebrews 2:1–3; 3:12–19; 6:4–6; 10:26–31). God spoke through Moses at Mout Sinai; those who disobeyed "did not escape" (Hebrews 12:25). How much more will be our punishment if we ignore the voice of Jesus who spoke on earth (see Hebrews 1:2) and continues to speak from heaven? Moses was just the transmitter (*chrēmatizein*, "warned") while what Jesus said was the direct speech of God (*lalein*).[51] To "refuse him who speaks" (Jesus; 12:25) has far more serious consequences. To turn away from Him (v. 25) and to drift away from His gospel is to turn towards the full force of God's wrath against sin.

The "whole mountain trembled violently" (Exodus 19:18). It was a warning to the Israelites of God's power and the serious consequences of disobeying God's law. **Now the gospel of Jesus has been perfectly revealed in Christ. The world's rejection of it will result in the terrifying shaking of "not only the earth but also the heavens" (Hebrews 12:26; Haggai 2:6).** This will happen in the future, when "what can be shaken" (all the visible aspects of the created universe) will be removed "so that what cannot be shaken may remain" (the invisible aspects connected to the kingdom of God; Hebrews 12:27). God will shake the entire universe to reveal "a kingdom that cannot be shaken"—the only reality that will remain standing when everything else lies in ruins. We are reminded of the two houses that Jesus referred to (Matthew 7:24–27). The house built on the rock represents the wise man who "hears these words of mine and puts them into practice" (v. 24), while the other house on sand represents the foolish man who "hears these words of mine and does not put them into practice"(v. 26). The house on the rock withstood the great storm while the other house "fell with a great crash" (v. 27).

Those who listen to Christ who speaks, and obey accordingly, "are receiving a kingdom that cannot be shaken" (Hebrews 12:28). The phrase "are receiving" shows it is already happening now, and will continue until the kingdom is fully received. Therefore, we must worship God with eternal gratitude and "reverence and awe" (v. 28)—better translated as "godly fear". The writer throws another thunderbolt at his readers by quoting Deuteronomy 4:24, "God is a consuming fire".[52] We must tremble at His word and obey Him.

[51] Barclay, "The Letter to the Hebrews", 188.
[52] Ibid., 189.

ThinkThrough

Is it possible to refuse Jesus when He speaks to us? How is He speaking to you, and what is your response to what you hear Him say to you?

What does it mean in daily life when we say that we belong to this unshakeable kingdom? What other kingdoms vie for our attention and loyalty?

Day 54

Read Hebrews 13:1–3

How does one obey Jesus? The author of Hebrews provides three examples of what we can do to "make level paths for your feet" (Hebrews 12:13). First, we are urged, "Keep on loving one another as brothers and sisters" (13:1). This is what Jesus taught His disciples (John 13:34–35) and what the apostles continued to teach (1 Thessalonians 4:9; 1 John 3:11–12, 23). **Such love does not depend on whether we like others or not, but on the fact that we share the same heavenly Father.** It involves a deep commitment and practical expression (1 John 3:17). "Mutual affection" (2 Peter 1:7) would be a mark of maturing faith and it should characterise relationships in the church.

Second, we are urged to be hospitable (Hebrews 13:2). Love helps us to respond to others with Christian hospitality. The writer tells his readers not to forget "to show hospitality to strangers" and that some people have in the past "shown hospitality to angels without knowing it" (v. 2; see Genesis 18:1–15; 19:1–3). Jesus will one day say to the faithful, "I was a stranger and you invited me in", something that may surprise them because they were not aware of it (Matthew 25:35, 38). Christian hospitality was often a necessary virtue in the early church because visiting preachers needed accommodation other than the public inns (often dirty places of ill-repute). Thus, Christians were urged to welcome brothers even if they did not know them personally (see 3 John 5–8; Romans 12:13). Hospitality was one of the qualifications for church leadership (1 Timothy 3:2; Titus 1:8).

Third, we should empathise with those who are suffering and in need (Hebrews 13:3). Christian love will express itself in compassionate acts towards needy people. Here, the writer refers to those in prison, most likely believers who were imprisoned for their faith, or those who were reduced to poverty through systematic persecution and thrown into jail as debtors. These brothers should not be forgotten, but visited with care and supported prayerfully. Jesus will one day commend the faithful, "I was in prison and you came to visit me" (Matthew 25:36). When Paul was imprisoned in Rome (most likely for the second time), many deserted him (2 Timothy 1:15). But Onesiphorus, his friend and fellow worker, visited him with food and water, the supply of which prisoners were left to find for themselves (2 Timothy 1:16–18). Empathy for those mistreated ("as if you yourselves were suffering" (Hebrews 13:3; see Isaiah 63:9, where God shows such empathy) is an expression of true Christian love.

The author uses the phrase "keep on loving" (Hebrews 13:1)— what does that mean? When may we be tempted to give up loving? How is this love expressed through hospitality? What would Christian hospitality look like today?

How can we grow in our empathy for those who are suffering and in need? Make a list of people you know who may need an encouraging word, a concerned visit, or supportive prayer. Turn it into a "to-do" list.

Day 55

Read Hebrews 13:4–6

Two further exhortations are made here regarding living rightly in the midst of persecution and suffering. The Christian must depart from sexual immorality and greed. Instead, he should pursue holiness and contentment. Marriage was instituted by God (Genesis 2:18, 24; Matthew 19:6) and should be recognised as an honourable estate. This is shown by both husband and wife remaining faithful to each other, as they promised when they got married. Others should also recognise this lifelong relationship and not do anything that may wreck it. The "marriage bed" must be "kept pure" (Hebrews 13:4). This means sexual relationship within a marriage is not dirty or sinful (unlike some wrong teaching that considered it sinful; see 1 Timothy 4:3), and it is kept pure by keeping out adultery and all kinds of sexual immorality (Hebrews 13:4). God will judge those guilty of sexual misbehaviour as it is against God's purposes. The existence of Christian marriages in a world that operates on sexual permissiveness faces increasing challenges. This requires Christians to take their marriage seriously. Churches must also take responsibility to exhort, teach, and support marriages and families.

Greed is another major problem in our materialistic world. The world has become one big shopping centre and entertainment complex. To enjoy the things of the world, one becomes greedy for money, which is used to purchase goods and experiences. But greed is considered in Scripture as idolatry (Ephesians 5:5; Colossians 3:5) because it is tantamount to the worship of money rather than God (Matthew 6:24). Paul warns how greed leads men to pursue "many foolish and harmful desires that plunge people into ruin and destruction" (1 Timothy 6:9). Indeed, "the love of money is a root of all kinds of evil" (v. 10) and the antidote for it is "godliness with contentment" (v. 6). Dangerous greed can be seen in so many places today—in shopping centres, stock markets, casinos, and glittering streets of sinful consumption.

Contentment that keeps a man godly comes from knowledge of Scripture and commitment to its truth.

Here two passages are quoted: Deuteronomy 31:6 and Psalm 118:6–7, both assuring us of God's enabling presence that knows our needs and provides for them. Trusting in God for His provision is a mark of faithful discipleship that refuses to be enticed by the seductive temptations of the sinful world, but lives steadily with godliness and contentment.

Reflect on the
two promises in
Hebrews 13:5–6.
How would they
help the believer to
remain godly and
contented?

What does this
passage say about
how you are living?
What does it say
about your thoughts,
imagination, words,
habits, desires,
relationships, and
choices? Is there
anything that needs
your thoughtful and
prayerful action?

Day 56

Read Hebrews 13:7–8

One of the greatest joys of an aging teacher is to meet former students who have now become important people, but who greet their teachers with love, gratitude, and reverence. Here the writer urges his readers to "remember" their former teachers and leaders (Hebrews 13:7). The word for "remember", *mnēmoneuō*, means to hold in memory, keep in mind, and cherish. The people to be remembered were former leaders who had taught and mentored others in the church. Many had by now departed (note the word "spoke" in v. 7, which denotes an action in the past), but they continued to inspire those who remembered them, what they taught (the Word of God), how they lived ("the outcome of their way of life"), and their faith (v. 7). Such faithful and exemplary teachers continued to influence their former students even if they were no longer around. The saying "God buries his workmen, but he carries on his work" is so apt here.[53] **The life and teachings of those who have taught and mentored us, whose godliness and love for God continue to stand out as a testimony of God's grace, must be remembered.** Not only are we to remember our personal or corporate mentors, such as former pastors and teachers in the church, we must also learn to rediscover an illustrious line of great teachers throughout church history, such as the church fathers, the reformers, pastors, theologians, missionaries, and preachers. There is a great need to remember great Christian biography and the history of Christian doctrine and devotion.

These people have left behind an outstanding heritage, and we would do well to emulate and be inspired by them. We are to "imitate their faith" (Hebrews 13:7; see 6:12; 11:2) so that we end up imitating Christ (1 Corinthians 11:1; 1 Peter 2:21; 1 John 2:6). We remember well when we realise that God's purpose is that we be conformed to the image of His Son (Romans 8:29).

This brings our attention to the ultimate leader (the Head; Colossians 1:18) in the church— the Lord Jesus Christ. All faithful leaders and teachers follow the Lord Jesus Christ. It is not possible to be a godly leader without being a faithful follower of Christ. He is "the same yesterday and today and for ever" (Hebrews 13:8; see 1:12; Psalm 102:27). Hence all godly leaders who are faithful followers of Jesus would be faithful to His character, grace, and purposes, which are unchanging.

[53] Stedman, *Hebrews*, 153.

Make a list of those who have mentored and taught you. What do you remember of their life and teachings? Thank God for them. Who are you presently teaching and mentoring?

Remembering our mentors should lead us to remember Jesus. In what way are you imitating Jesus? How does the truth of the unchanging Jesus help you to remain faithful to Him?

Day 57

Read Hebrews 13:9–16

This passage is not easy to understand as the author refers to "all kinds of strange teachings" (literally "many-colored")[54] that were presumably circulating in the church (Hebrews 13:9). We can only guess what some of these were. The author mentions ceremonial foods (see Leviticus 11); it is likely that some people were practising the old Jewish dietary laws believing that doing so would be spiritually edifying. The author refutes such thinking by saying that it is "of no benefit" (Hebrews 13:9). We are not spiritually strengthened by material food; only by God's grace.

The writer also refers to the fact that on the Day of Atonement, the priest had "no right to eat" the meat of the sacrificial animals (Hebrews 13:10). This must be totally consumed by fire outside the camp (v. 11; see Leviticus 16:27). Bible commentator William Barclay conjectures that some people might have been teaching (wrongly) that the bread eaten at the Lord's Supper actually became the body of Christ.[55] Whatever the case may be, the author turns our attention to the fact that Christ was crucified and offered as a sacrifice outside Jerusalem (fulfilling the Old Testament practice in Leviticus 16:27). We are to go to Him outside the camp (meaning we have to leave popular practices

that are unbiblical so that we can truly turn to Christ and His sacrifice).

Jesus bore the disgrace and we must do the same (Hebrews 13:13, see Luke 9:23). The author adds the note that our salvation lies outside the earthly Jerusalem (and the temple rituals in it; Hebrews 13:13). Instead, our hearts must be turned to the "enduring city", the "city that is to come" (v. 14; see 11:10, 16). **Our faith must rise above the horizons of ritualistic religion to Christ our Saviour.**

We are urged to offer a different kind of sacrifice, "a sacrifice of praise" (Hebrews 13:15). Not only must our faith be that of profession of praise, but we must also offer Christ our obedient and faith-filled deeds. Two are mentioned here: doing good and practising generosity ("share with others", v. 16). Glorifying God in worship, good deeds done to others, and showing generosity to those in need—these are sacrifices that God is pleased with (v. 16).

[54] Morris, "Hebrews", 149.
[55] Barclay, "The Letter to the Hebrews", 197.

What strange teachings are you aware that may be circulating among Christians today? Assess them in the light of Scripture.

Reflect on how you are glorifying and praising God, doing good, and practising generosity. Is there any area where you can, by God's grace, do these more and more?

Day 58

Read Hebrews 13:17–19

While Hebrews 13:7–8 deals with past leaders, this passage deals with those who were still serving. What should be the attitude of believers towards their spiritual leaders in church? Here the author urges, "Have confidence in your leaders and submit to their authority" (Hebrews 13:17). This is not a prescription for abuse of power and authority in the church (see Mark 10:42–43; 2 Corinthians 1:24; 1 Peter 5:3; 3 John 9–10). The style of leadership that Jesus prescribes is servant leadership. Jesus, "knowing that the Father had given all things into his hands" (John 13:3 ESV), began to wash His disciples' feet with those hands. Authority is to be used for service. Note that this authority is not native, but conferred on them by the Lord. That is why in such relationships we are to submit "as [we] do to the Lord" (see Ephesians 5:22; 6:1, 5). By disobeying authorities placed over us, we are actually disobeying and dishonouring God, to whom they (and we) "must give an account" (Hebrews 13:17). Such submission and obedience does not come easy in a modern culture which celebrates independence and equality and the authority of the self, more than other authorities.

Respecting our God-appointed spiritual leaders

not only honours God, but also makes the work of the leaders a joy instead of being a painful burden (Hebrews 13:17). The author points out that disobedience would not be of any help to the church. It is proper to respect and submit to godly leaders who serve God with a clear conscience, and who "desire to live honourably in every way" (v. 18). It is neither fair nor proper to make the lives of such leaders difficult by a rebellious spirit, the way the Israelites made it difficult for Moses (Exodus 5:20–22; 16:2; 17:2; Numbers 14:1–4; 20:3).

Instead of causing unnecessary difficulties for our spiritual leaders, we are called to keep praying for them (Hebrews 13:18).[56] The writer asks for prayer for himself (v. 19). A similar request was made by Paul (Ephesians 6:19; Colossians 4:3; 1 Thessalonians 5:25; 2 Thessalonians 3:1). It is important to pray for our leaders because in their work for the Lord, they often encounter intense spiritual struggle as they face opposition from Satan, the unbelieving world, and the self (see Romans 15:30). Our prayers make a significant difference in their lives.

[56] Morris, "Hebrews", 153.

ThinkThrough

How should one obey and submit to spiritual leaders? How can we avoid both the extremes of blind obedience and refusal to submit to spiritual leaders? Assess your own attitudes and actions in this light.

Make a list of spiritual leaders in your life. What can you pray for them? Do you think it would help them to know that you are praying for them?

Day 59

Read Hebrews 13:20–21

This closing benediction "must rank among the most powerfully worded blessings found in Scripture".[57] It asks for God's blessings on His people so that they thrive in His grace and love. "God of peace" (Hebrews 13:20) refers to the mission of God to bring peace to our broken and alienated lives. Paul echoes the phrase (Romans 15:33; 16:20), reminding us that God's redemptive intervention in our lives brings us peace with God (Romans 5:1) and with one another (Ephesians 2:14–16). God achieves our salvation through His Son Jesus Christ, "that great Shepherd of the sheep" (Hebrews 13:20) who, as our great and unique High Priest, "lays down his life for the sheep" (John 10:11). The blood shed by Jesus is the "blood of the eternal covenant" (Hebrews 13:20; see 8:10). This is the better covenant that surpasses the earlier one (7:22), replacing the old religious rituals and law with the reality of Christ.

Though Jesus died, God raised Him from the dead (Hebrews 13:20, the first direct reference to the resurrection in this book; see 1:3; 7:11, 15–16), thus proving Christ and His claims to be true. The resurrected Jesus is alive and present in our lives as He reigns above, being seated at the Father's right hand. We can trust Him as He watches over us in His sovereign grace. God is presently at "work in us" (v. 21), something many Christians forget or neglect. As God works in us, He equips us "with everything good" (v. 21). And will God our heavenly Father ever refuse us such good gifts (Matthew 7:11)?

The purpose of this equipping (the word implies mending)[58] is that we may please God by doing His will (Hebrews 13:21). God's will is that we should "be conformed to the image of his Son" (Romans 8:29) and that "in all things at all times, having all that you need, you will abound in every good work" (2 Corinthians 9:8; see Hebrews 13:15–16) that God in His grace has "prepared in advance for us to do" (Ephesians 2:10). **We have all we need in Christ so that we can live life fully for God's glory and please Him in every way.**

[57] Stedman, *Hebrews*, 157.
[58] Morris, "Hebrews", 155.

ThinkThrough

Reflect on what the God of peace has done for us. What does all this mean for you personally?

What roles do Jesus and the Spirit play in your blessings? What does doing God's will mean for you today?

Day 60

Read Hebrews 13:22–25

Though Hebrews begins like a sermon it ends like a letter, with greetings and final salutations. The writer remains unidentified. He urges his readers to "bear with my word of exhortation" (Hebrews 13:22). Though he has written to them "quite briefly" (but not that briefly when compared to many of the other epistles in the New Testament; v. 22), he hopes that his readers would take his exhortations and warnings seriously. **Throughout the letter, he has urged his Jewish Christian readers not to drift away from Christ. Neither fear of persecution nor weakening of devotion to Christ must lead them astray, especially to return to the old Judaism of their forefathers.** Such a move would rob them of the reality that is in Christ; they would simply be moving back to lifeless shadows that in effect point to Christ our true High Priest and perfect sacrifice for our sins and mediator of the new and perfect covenant. The writer has written with great burden and passion. He hopes that his letter would make a difference in ensuring faith, holiness, and Christ-honouring deeds among his readers (including us).

A reference is made to Timothy (most likely the protégé and associate of Paul; Hebrews 13:23). Timothy had suffered imprisonment and had just been released. Perhaps he was thrown into prison through Alexander, the man Paul warned him about (2 Timothy 4:14–15). Timothy served in Ephesus and knew many people in Asia Minor and nearby provinces. It is possible that the recipients of Hebrews were Christian Jews living in these areas and knew Timothy. The author expresses his hopes to visit his readers with Timothy. Italy is mentioned, but it is not the place from where the author wrote the epistle. Note that he mentions those "from" (not "in") Italy (Hebrews 13:24).

The writer sends greetings to "all your leaders"—the third time he uses the term (Hebrews 13:24, see vv. 7, 17). This shows his special respect for church leaders. The term "all the Lord's people" refers to all the groups of Christians (churches) in the area. The word "all" offers greetings in an inclusive way. The letter ends with the signature phrase, "Grace be with you all" (v. 25), reminiscent of how the apostle Paul ended some of his letters (Colossians 4:18; 2 Thessalonians 3:18; Titus 3:15). This is a fitting way to end a letter that focuses on God's grace fully available in the gospel of Jesus Christ, "the one and only Son" (John 1:14, 18). We are to draw near to Christ and stay close to Him.

The writer of Hebrews urged his readers to bear with his word of exhortation. How can we take his exhortations and warnings seriously? Think of a specific application for your life.

Hebrews ends with a note on grace. What does the book say about the throne of grace to which we now have access through Christ (Hebrews 4:16)? Thank God for the grace that comes to us through and in Christ.

Going Deeper
in Your Walk with Christ

Whether you're a new Christian or have been a Christian for a while, it's worth taking a journey through the gospels of Matthew, Mark, Luke, and John. Each gospel presents a distinct aspect of Christ and helps us gain a deeper appreciation of who Jesus is, why He came, and what it means for us.

Hear His words. Witness His works. Deepen your walk with Jesus as you follow Him through the wonderful scenes painted in the gospels.

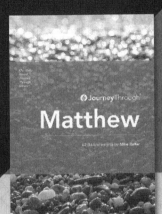

JourneyThrough
Matthew
Mike Raiter

JourneyThrough
Mark
Robert M. Solomon

JourneyThrough
Luke
Mike Raiter

JourneyThrough
John
David Cook

Journey Through
Act

The book of Acts is one of the most exciting parts of the Bible. Jesus has just ascended to heaven, the Spirit has come to the church, and we see God at work building the church and causing the gospel message to spread through Judea, into Samaria, throughout Asia, into Europe, and finally to Rome. Despite opposition from religious and commercial interests and dissension within the church, the gospel will progress and people will come to Christ.

Embark on a daily journey through the book of Acts, and see how the Holy Spirit empowers the church to witness in ever widening circles until the gospel reaches the ends of the earth.

David Cook was Principal of the Sydney Missionary and Bible College for 26 years. He is an accomplished writer and has authored Bible commentaries, books on the Minor Prophets, and several Bible study guides.

Journey Through
Romans

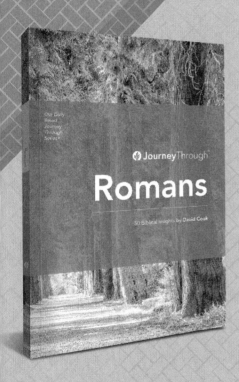

The book of Romans outlines what Christians believe and explains God's perfect plan in bringing sinners back to Him. More than any other book in the Bible, it has played a crucial role in shaping church history, and has been called the greatest theological document ever written. Many have found Romans a daunting book to study. But David Cook writes in a style that makes difficult truths easy to understand. Rediscover why the gospel is such good news, and walk away with a deeper appreciation of what and why you believe.

David Cook was Principal of the Sydney Missionary and Bible College for 26 years. He is an accomplished writer and has authored Bible commentaries, books on the Minor Prophets, and several Bible study guides.

ABOUT THE PUBLISHER

Discovery House Publishing™
produces a wide array of premium
and quality resources that focus on Scripture,
show reverence for God and His Word,
demonstrate the relevance of vibrant faith,
and equip and encourage you to draw closer
to God in all seasons of your life.

Discovery House
P u b l i s h i n g™

NOTE TO THE READER

We invite you to share your response to the message of this book by writing to us at:

5 Pereira Road #07-01
Asiawide Industrial Building
Singapore 368025

or sending an email to:

dhpsingapore@dhp.org

Made in the USA
Middletown, DE
15 May 2024

54377365R00077